LET THE ANCIE
TRANSFORM Y

They are the cos............................ es
upon which the great pyramids of Egypt were
built—and the natural superconductors
through which a universe of enlightenment
passed to the lost continent of Atlantis.

Now you too can tune in to the ancient and
futuristic powers of magical, mystical crystals,
using sapphire, rose quartz, clear quartz,
emerald, and other gemstones to facilitate
healing, energize the mind, and illuminate
every facet of your highest potential. Your
eyes will open to a wondrous new vision of
you!

THE
CRYSTAL
HANDBOOK

KEVIN SULLIVAN is a New Yorker who has
been using crystals for years. An avid student
of crystal lore, he has even prospected for the
magical minerals—thus allowing his most
prized specimens ample opportunity to find
him.

EVOKE THE WISDOM OF THE TAROT

With your own set of 78, full-color cards—the Rider-Waite deck—you will learn to unlock the secrets of the Tarot and understand their mysterious and beautiful symbols.

THE
CRYSTAL
HANDBOOK

KEVIN SULLIVAN

An Armadillo Press Book

A SIGNET BOOK

NEW AMERICAN LIBRARY

NAL BOOKS ARE AVAILABLE AT QUANTITY DISCOUNTS WHEN USED
TO PROMOTE PRODUCTS OR SERVICES. FOR INFORMATION PLEASE
WRITE TO PREMIUM MARKETING DIVISION, NEW AMERICAN LIBRARY,
1633 BROADWAY, NEW YORK, NEW YORK 10019.

SIGNET, SIGNET CLASSIC, MENTOR, ONYX, PLUME,
MERIDIAN and NAL BOOKS are published by NAL PEN-
GUIN INC., 1633 Broadway, New York, New York 10019

First Printing, December, 1987

1 2 3 4 5 6 7 8 9

PRINTED IN THE UNITED STATES OF AMERICA

To my parents,
who have always been dedicated to me

CONTENTS

AN INTRODUCTION TO CRYSTALS   13

THE ENCYCLOPEDIA OF CRYSTALS   25

USING YOUR CRYSTAL OR GEMSTONE   153
  Choosing a Crystal of Gemstone (and a
    Crystal or Gemstone Store)   155
  Cleansing Your Crystal   159
  Getting to Know Your Crystal   160
  Selecting Stones for Others   161
  Losing a Crystal   161
  Placing Your Crystals   162
  Body Work—Meditation Exercises   166
  Mini-Exercises for Quick Stress Relief   169
  Pets and Crystals   171
  The Erotic Crystal   173
  Storing Crystals   176

SPENDING A DAY WITH YOUR
  CRYSTAL   179

BIRTHSTONES   191

CRYSTAL GAZING   199

CHARTS FOR INSTANT REFERENCE   207
  Zodiac Affinities   209
  Stones for Any Sign   210
  Stones and Their Signs by Color   211
  Wear to Wear Crystals   212
  Mental and Emotional Influences of
    Crystals   213
  Crystals to Help You in Your Profession   219

GLOSSARY   222

Acknowledgments:

Special thanks go to:

Betty Anne Crawford
Snowdon Parlette III
Teresa Kennedy
Sid Kaplan
Astro Minerals Limited, New York City
Gemstoned, New York City
Mitchell Netburn
Luis Mora
Scott Plunkett
Susan Herner
Matt Sartwell
Alex Tanous
Sarah Shmitt
Sandra Lipson
Kerry Harvestine
James at Freebeing
Irving and Robert Katz

He builded better than he knew;—
The conscious stone to beauty grew.
                    —Emerson, *The Problem*

Similia Similubus Curantur (Like Cures
Like).
        —Hahnemann, motto for homeopathy

AN
INTRODUCTION
TO
CRYSTALS

Gemstones have fascinated mankind since prehistoric times. Beyond their intrinsic beauty, these special crystals can somehow focus the miraculous hidden energy of the universe, energy that can be directed toward spiritual awareness and realization. Indeed, the ancients found that certain gemstones, worn originally for their decorative value, seemed to bring a peace of mind to the wearer. Later they realized that the magic stones could even affect bodily healing. They began to study and collect information on the stones. Much of this valuable data has been lost to us in the past few centuries as our attentions have turned away from spiritual life to more worldly concerns. We have expended our valuable energy building technology and empires, which can serve us only during our brief worldly encounter, and have ignored the vast time we must spend elsewhere.

Miraculously, and to our good fortune, some of this priceless information has recently been recovered. New disclosures on the effects of gemstones have been made available through trance "channelers," who have brought back to us information lost thousands, even millions of years ago. ("Channeling," a recently publicized phenomenon, is a process whereby a psychic enters a deep state of meditation and allows his or her consciousness to be temporarily set aside so that other, more evolved souls may enter the body and use it to communicate information. The channeler often has no conscious recall of the information discussed while in a trance, necessitating the presence of a scribe so that the information can be recorded.)

Although many of the beneficial effects of gemstones are not directly explainable by our limited knowledge of the physical world, we do know that all gemstones possess a crystalline structure. Crystalline structures can collect, focus, and emit electromagnetic energy. In fact, the physical properties of crystals, both natural and man-made, are fascinating in and of themselves, and are yet to be fully explored.

Even though our scientific understanding of crystals is incomplete, we have learned to put the power of crystals to practical use in many ways. We cannot go through our day without coming into contact with the emissions of a nearby man-made crystal. Crystals transmit and receive radio waves, power our quartz watches, set the timing on our home computers, and even release the sound energies recorded on our favorite records.

But what is this power? How does it work? Scientists have long known that a crystal set in an energy field will collect and focus that energy. They also know that if a crystal is squeezed, it will release its own internal energy (the piezoelectric effect). Yet science is not even close to understanding how truly powerful crystals are in the more important task of focusing *life energy*. This power, not explainable by physical laws, is nonetheless revealed by the way crystals focus ordinary energy.

Of all the natural crystals, Quartz is perhaps the master gemstone. It is found throughout the world on every continent and has long been noted for its special healing properties. Chemically, Quartz is composed of silicon and oxygen (SiO_2), a combination known to geologists as the building block of minerals. In fact, most of our planet is made up of minerals containing SiO_2. Silicon dioxide is also an important constituent of our body, which may be the physical basis for our connection to crystals. The transfer of energy from the natural crystal to our body's silicon could have something to do with healing.

Quartz was one of the first crystals to be intensely studied for both its spiritual and technological properties. It was the first crystal used to transmit and receive radio waves, and it was also the first gemstone to be synthesized. Quartz made possible the computer revolution. (It is what makes up our electronic chips, or integrated circuits, as they are more properly known.) But some believe Quartz has other, far more important abilities. For instance, the effects of acupuncture are reported to be increased by ten to twelve percent when the needles are coated with quartz crystal. Quartz also enhances muscle testing and protects individuals from certain kinds of radiation. These are only the known properties. <u>Much more needs to be learned about this powerful absorber and emitter, capable of both protecting the body and nourishing it by regulating energy flows.</u> But, fortunately, it is not necessary to completely understand this remarkable gemstone in order to gain its benefits. Simply obtaining a proper stone allows you to experience and enjoy its remarkable powers. It is, like many other gemstones, effective either when worn or just placed about the household or work area.

A great deal of folklore exists on the use of gemstones as good luck charms, talismans, and healing agents. This folklore contains valuable information because so much of it is accurate. Almost all ancient societies use gemstones in some way, either for healing or spiritual enhancement. Even today we practice some of these ancient customs without even being aware that we are doing it. For example, the use of the engagement ring is one of the more common ways gemstones are employed as talismans. Other talismans such as bells, bracelets, earrings, necklaces, signets, and seals may include crystals in their design to give added power. Without even being aware of it, we are purposely experiencing the effects of crystals. Many people don't feel comfortable unless they are wearing their favorite ring or piece of jewelry incorporating a specific gemstone, and yet they don't know why they feel that way.

Traditionally gemstones have often been

used in conjunction with various planets and constellations of the zodiac. The use of birthstones expresses the ancient belief that certain stones bring luck and protection. But birthstones actually offer a way to link the cosmic forces of the sky with the crystal energies of the earth in order to exploit the maximum power of both. Astrological forces' interlink with gemstone crystal energy because, in their positioning and exposure to the planets, gemstones absorb and store particular resonances. They are, in a sense, a way of "tuning" your individual body to the flow of energy through the universe.

Birthstones are important as primary receivers and can occasionally amplify the power of certain other crystals on our body and within our spiritual field. The gemstones associated with different zodiac signs have the ability to isolate and store direct stellar influences. They also allow other influences to pass through them, amplifying or eliminating those powers according to how their interference patterns interact within the crystal structure.

Exposure to the various birthstone crystals can enhance health within any individual, even those not born under a particular sign. The qualities are maximized by, but not limited to, those born in a particular house. Health may be promoted within the physical form by the isolation of the property associated with each gemstone. Study the properties and qualities assigned to each stone according to popular astrological interpretations in order to understand what specific benefits may be gained.

Each mineral crystal listed in this encyclopedia has its special influence, function, and vibration. Inherent within the evolution of the mineral kingdom are the vibratory rates that heal, energize, attune, and uplift the spirit of our inner beings. There are no two crystals exactly alike, as there are no two identical snowflakes. The place and time of their forming and the energies present in the earth and in the cosmos affect their creation and give them particular qualities, just as the chemical impurities and atomic radiation present at their birth imbue them with individual color and luster. As a result, each gem or mineral emits its unique musical "note." This can be heard by discerning ears, especially in the proximity of large mineral collections.

The energy emitted by gemstones can be tapped as long as the wearer chooses to make use of the stone. Natural gemstones do not lose their power with age or use. Their energy comes from the cosmos and, once activated, is eternal. It should also be noted that natural gemstones and crystals are stronger in their powers than those that are man-made. Although what is made by man in clinical and sterile workshops can be just as beautiful and marvelous to behold, in the last analysis, synthetic gems cannot compete with what is devised and given physical manifestation by the laws of the universe. Gems formed artificially are made too quickly to accurately absorb and attune themselves to the vibrations of the universe. They are mere snapshots compared to powerful natural stones formed over millions of years.

Many of the concepts being outlined here may at first seem overwhelming to the novice interested in tapping the power of crystals. Fortunately, however, gemstone crystals work on the body of the wearer and in the household or workplace regardless of whether or not their properties are understood by the user. Still, the properties can be influenced by the minds of those involved in the making or wearing of any item indicated, and an understanding of the proper use of these powerful stones is important. Never forget that their misuse can have consequences as well. If you are not sure of the properties of a particular stone, check with an expert before accepting it into your life.

Much folklore speaks of good luck and bad. With crystals, however, there is no such thing as a lucky or unlucky stone. In some areas of the world, magnetic force fields around certain gems and pieces of jewelry are created for the purpose of personal domination and imposition of one's will over another. But mostly, we are led or attracted to a certain gem or crystal, consciously or unconsciously, to seek some form of vibrational additive that in many cases can be supplied only by the specific gem or mineral. Many people see a stone and experience a sudden impulsive desire to own it. They don't know why, but they want to have that particular gem in their possession, either to carry in their pocket or to wear on their hand or around their neck. When this occurs there is generally a need for that particular gemstone's vibrational additive. Even when you consciously attempt to select a crystal, during handling one or more crystals will always seem "right" for your own reasons. This should be respected. Although similar classes of crystals exhibit similiar qualities and therefore would all be expected to have the desired effect, the one selected by feel is usually the optimum for fulfilling the prevailing need.

Throughout our lives we live with and are affected by crystal energy whether we know it or not, and whether we like it or not. We have been generally guided to live in the geographical location of our daily existence by the effects of crystals. We are led to move toward or away from areas of high mineral content, as their vibrations are a constant additive to our auric field and unconsciously affect much of our daily routine. Certain spaces feel more comfortable to us than others, certain locations feel right and nurturing, and yet we cannot put our finger on why. Have you ever considered that this is because of local mineral formations interacting with your personal fields?

Gemstones are believed to affect the body by influencing the etheric web that lies just outside the field of vision. Human bodies are surrounded by an electromagnetic field that is sometimes visible in special pictures known as Kirlian photographs. This field can be, and often is, charged with electricity. We all know about walking on a carpet with rubber shoes and touching a ground source or another person. We receive a shock of static electricity conducted through our auric field. Gemstones also have their fields of electrical energy that, when worn on the body or carried in close proximity to a person, will affect the body of the person as well. The size and shape of the field is determined by how the mineral was formed. This is why synthetic gems are rarely as powerful or effective. They simply do not carry the same natural field of energy needed to assimilate with the complex aura of a living being. Although they may appear to work in a general way, the effects are likely to be incomplete in the same way that synthetic vitamins are incomplete. Man-made stones must remain, at best, a second choice. They do not contain all the myriad trace elements present in natural stones any more than synthetic vitamins contain all the complexity of the natural variety.

The final thing to remember about gemstones: they are not a panacea for all problems. They are guides that focus energies and help us get in touch with the universal forces that surround us. But they are not the forces themselves, merely the reflections of energies that are already present and are amplified and tuned for our use, not our misuse. Misuse of the powers guided into us by crystals can have negative consequences. Some believe that the civilization of Atlantis, said to have developed a high degree of understanding of crystal use, was destroyed as a result of misuse of this tremendous power. Use crystals wisely and sparingly, and remember that the goal is to obtain understanding of, and control over, your personal auric field. Eventually you will put aside the crystal, after it has done its work. It is not meant to be a permanent crutch but rather a guide and companion into the world of spiritual awareness.

THE
ENCYCLOPEDIA
OF
CRYSTALS

Abalone

Abalone is an organic seashell. The outside of the shell is generally shaded with gray or white, the inside with pink, orange, yellow, and white. Abalone is usually found in warm tropical seas off the coasts of South America, Japan, and China.

Abalone is used by athletes to help build and protect muscle tissue. The heart can also obtain beneficial effects from this shell. Although it has little direct effect on the digestive organs themselves, Abalone is said to aid digestion.

◇ ◇ ◇

Agate

Agates are members of the Chalcedony family and, as such, are composed of microscopic crystals of Quartz laid down in colorful bands or ribbons. The appearance of the stone is waxy and soft. They are almost always translucent and occasionally transparent. Agates form in many different parts of the world and are named either for their appearance or place of origin.

Agates are grounding stones that help

27

you obtain a better physical and emotional balance. They work to raise consciousness and lead us to accept ourselves more fully by building self-confidence. They are also an aid to the digestive system.

Botswana Agate

It should come as no surprise that this stone hails from the land of its namesake. It is gray and waxy in appearance. Although many people can benefit from this member of the Chalcedony family, it is strongly recommended for fire fighters, for people who smoke, and for anyone who comes in regular contact with excessive amounts of heat or smoke. It is particularly helpful for anyone who wants to quit smoking.

Botswana Agate is beneficial to the circulatory system, the skin, and the brain. This is because it has the ability to help the body assimilate oxygen more readily. A pleasant side effect may be giddiness (an increase of oxygen in the body makes you slightly light-headed and less prone to see things in a negative way). Depression is also soothed by Botswana Agate.

Botswana Agate has an affinity with Gemini.

Fire Agate

The identification of Fire Agate is a somewhat confusing and even controversial subject. Some consider it merely a form of

Carnelian. Others have categorized it as an Opal. In fact, Fire Agate and Carnelian are both members of the Chalcedony family, a possible source of some of the confusion. Nonetheless, Fire Agate does have distinct healing qualities and is considered a separate stone by experts. It is most often found in North America and comes in shades of orange, brown, blue, or green.

Perhaps the most important aspect of Fire Agate is its connection to the energies of the earth. Using Fire Agate is a calming experience and will help you feel more settled and secure. This makes it an excellent stone to use before meditating. It will help to mellow the user's existence and will induce a fine feeling of relaxation. As with other stones in tune with the earth, Fire Agate can benefit sexual endeavors. Fire Agate can also help alleviate problems relating to the stomach and endocrine system.

Oftentimes experts say that orange stones are highly stimulating and should be used with great care because of their ability to bring hidden problems to the surface. With Fire Agate this can be an advantage. Its grounding influence helps you examine and deal with the problems that well up in a calm and safe manner. Fire Agates can be worn anywhere on the body for any length of time and will always help to take the edge off difficult experiences.

Fire Agate has affinity with Aries, Leo, Virgo, Capricorn, and Gemini. It is recommended for dentists, optometrists, and those in the healing profession.

Moss Agate

Moss Agate is another member of the Chalcedony family. Generally these stones are black, blue, or brown and are found in the United States, Australia, and India. The most striking physical attribute of Moss Agate is its branched markings in brown, gray, or white that cover the surface of the stone like moss. By virtue of its connection to the earth and its organic-looking markings, Moss Agate is a wonderful stone for people involved with agriculture or botany. It is also of value to midwives.

Moss Agate is very beneficial for the cleansing and circulatory systems, and can help relieve depression by balancing the conflicts between the right and left sides of the brain. This stone can be especially useful to methodical people who have trouble getting in touch with their intuitive feelings. Moss Agate will help them to act with less personal restriction. It can also help intuitive or creative people channel their energies in a more practical way. It is helpful for hypoglycemia.

Moss Agate, as with all Agates, has an affinity for Geminis.

◊ ◊ ◊

Albite

Albite is a white or translucent stone with a bluish tinge. It is found in North America, England, France, Japan, and Kenya. Moonstones are a cut and polished form of Albite (*see Moonstone*).

Albite helps relieve depression and can be used as a booster for the immune and respiratory systems. It is also soothing for mental stress and strengthens the spleen and thymus.

Gem literature suggests that Albite's properties can be increased if it is placed under a pyramid with a Garnet, Ruby, or Emerald for fifteen to twenty minutes.

Albite, like Moonstone, has affinity with Cancer, Scorpio, and Pisces.

◊ ◊ ◊

Alexanderite

Alexanderite is a green stone, a form of Chrysoberyl that was discovered in the U.S.S.R. in the early nineteenth century and named for Czar Alexander II. Outside Russia it is found in Brazil and Sri Lanka. An unusual quality of Alexanderite is that the dark green stone shines red in transmitted light.

Alexanderite is beneficial to the nervous system, spleen, pancreas, and testes. But if a single attribute of Alexanderite had to be spotlighted, it would be its regenerative capabilities on both the mental as well as the physical planes. Alexanderite guides and assists you in rebuilding your self-respect. It helps you recognize your importance and worth in this world. It can also help you highlight your place in nature and your role in a healthy ecology.

Alexanderite soothes the emotions and can help wearers stabilize the expenditure of energy so that things that generally take great effort, whether mental or physical, are less taxing.

Alexanderite is given to people born in June as a birthstone.

Amazonite

Amazonite is a green stone instrumental in distilling the raw information you use for personal expression. It is a pale green form of Microcline, a potash feldspar, and is found in Brazil, U.S.S.R., and U.S. The best crystals are found near Pike's Peak. Contrary to what its name implies, it is not a product of the Amazon River.

Amazonite soothes the brain and nervous system, and helps you filter information and combine it with natural intuition. This can help find the most effective way of expression. Amazonite is also said to enhance masculine qualities and is good for anyone involved in the arts. It has an affinity with Virgo.

◇ ◇ ◇

Amber

Amber is composed of fossilized resin that formed millions of years ago from the sap of primeval trees. Amber often contains within it mummified insects or plant matter, which add to its connection to early life on this planet. Amber has been known and used by civilizations around the world for thousands of years, and in ancient times was highly prized for its talismanic powers. It ranges in color from a pale yellow to orange or dark brown. It can be opaque or transparent. Some of the darker clear types look like honey.

Although Amber is beneficial when used on any part of the body, it has especially good effects on the brain, lungs, thyroid, spleen, endocrine system, inner ear, and neurological tissue. It draws disease out of afflicted areas and neutralizes negative energy. Amber is a grounding healer in harmony with the energies of the earth. When used properly, Amber has the power to add stability to your life.

With its ability to draw out negative energy, Amber allows the body to heal itself. Having once been an organic entity, it gives its abilities quite readily to other organic entities. Amber maintains a harmonious balance between opposing elements. For this reason it is helpful in clearing up depression and bringing about a positive mental state. It is also useful as a memory aid.

Amber can be carried in your pocket, but it is best worn on the wrist. Its healing properties can be applied to any part of the body. Gem literature recommends that Amber be cleansed after being used for healing to dispense the negative energy it has absorbed. (See the chapter on general use of crystals for how to cleanse amber, or any crystal.)

As fossilized organic matter, Amber is in harmony with Abalone, Jet, Petrified Wood, and, to lesser extent, Marble and Obsidian.

Amber folklore is extensive, probably because the stone was so plentiful. It was the first substance used by man for decoration and is found in Stone Age deposits as talismans or amulets.

The Greek poets claimed grains of Amber were the tears shed over the death of Phaëthon by the Heliades after they had become poplars growing on the banks of the Eridanus. Sophocles explained the origin of Amber as the tears shed over the death of Meleager by Indian birds.

Nicias explained Amber as being the "juice" of the brilliant rays of the setting sun that were congealed in the sea and then cast up upon the shore. Ovid suggests Amber was the solidified urine of the lynx. In Viennese esoteric literature, deposits of

Amber marked the resting place of the spirit or spirits believed to animate the stone.

Whatever its origins, Amber was easily worked by primitive peoples and became a favorite object of trade and barter for the peoples of the Baltic coast. It was a popular Roman ornament and, ingeniously carved into animal forms, has been discovered as far north as Norway.

Marked or carved Amber was greatly esteemed, especially when the markings suggested the initials of the name of some prominent person. Those who secured Amber so mysteriously marked by nature's hand probably felt that they had obtained a talisman of great power, especially destined for their use.

Its zodiacal affinity is with Leo, Virgo, and Capricorn. Amber is recommended for chiropractors and masseurs.

◊ ◊ ◊

Amethyst

(See Quartz.)

◊ ◊ ◊

Apatite

Apatite is a mineral that is still in its embryonic stage as a healer. It gets its name from the Greek word meaning "to deceive" because it comes in so many forms and colors, and is easily confused with half a dozen other minerals. Apatite is found in transparent, translucent, and opaque forms, and varies in color from white to brown to green to yellow and even violet. Its crystal form is hexagonal and glassy in appearance. Apatite is found all over North America as well as in Mexico, Norway, U.S.S.R., and Sri Lanka. Apatite is most commonly confused with Fluorite and Aquamarine.

Muscle tissue will benefit from Apatite, as will general motor skills. It is suspected that since Apatite has a high calcium content it also promotes calcium absorption.

Apatite eases hypertension and restores clear thought.

Apatite as jewelry is best worn at the earlobes or on the thumb.

◇ ◇ ◇

Aquamarine

Aquamarine is a clear, blue-green gemstone that, like Emerald, is a form of Beryl. It is found in the United States, Mexico, U.S.S.R., Brazil, and India. Because of its soothing influence, eyeglasses were once made from Aquamarines. The stone also occurs in a golden yellow color.

Aquamarine is known for its ability to stabilize and harmonize unsettled surroundings. It filters out unnecessary information to the brain, calms the nerves, clarifies perception, and strengthens the body's cleansing organs such as the liver, spleen, thyroid, and kidneys. The eyes, jaw, neck, stomach, teeth, and throat are all helped by Aquamarine. It was given to sailors as protection against drowning and for courage in battle.

Aquamarine helps reduce fears and has a particular affinity with sensitive and mystical people. It increases creativity and sharpens intuition, enabling you to better interpret your emotions. It is an excellent stone for meditation and will help attune you to nature. It quiets the mind and reduces stress. It will also help bring about a tolerance toward others that balances all levels of your own personality.

It is recommended as a purifier of the throat and helps sore throats. It clears blocked communication and aids the user in verbal expression.

Copper has similar strengths to Aquamarine and when Aquamarine is put into direct sunlight with copper for eight to twenty-four hours, the filtering capabilities are intensified.

In ancient and medieval times, Aquamarine, like other blue stones, was believed to exercise a general tonic influence. It was also supposed to counteract the wiles of the spirits of darkness and procure the aid and favor of the spirits of light and wisdom. Sometimes it was looked upon as an emblem of chastity.

Aquamarine has an affinity with Aquar-

ius, Pisces, Taurus, Libra, and Scorpio. It
is a birthstone for March.

Aquamarine is a good stone for teachers,
councilors, chiropractors, genetic engi-
neers, lecturers, and massage practitioners.

Atacamite

Atacamite is a little-known crystal found in
Australia, Mexico, and Chile. It comes in
many shades of green and is transparent or
translucent. It occurs both as a prismatic,
single crystal and as an aggregate.

The genitals will benefit most from Atacamite, and it has a good effect on the thyroid gland and nervous system. Some
people claim that Atacamite has helped
them to be more resistant to herpes and
other venereal diseases.

Aventurine
(See Quartz.)

◊ ◊ ◊

Azurite   NE - OSE

Azurite is a blue, copper-based stone usually found in association with Malachite, which is its cousin. It is less common than Malachite but is found in abundance in Arizona.

Azurite is a dynamic and important stone, historically referred to as the jewel of wisdom. The priests and priestesses of ancient Egypt used this stone to enhance their spiritual consciousness. Famed psychic Edgar Cayce spoke of its ability to help him gain mental control and attain a meditative state more easily. Azurite is also said to increase psychic abilities.

Esoteric gem literature states that Azurite can restructure molecules, revitalize the brain, rebuild gray matter, and aid in developing embryonic babies in the womb.

The deep blue stone can help you release the past and gracefully anticipate and accept the future simultaneously, gaining a better understanding of your life. Azurite cultivates the ability to reach into the subconscious and objectively examine states of mind. This cleanses the mind and makes you more capable of insight and pure thought. Azurite helps you recognize the resources within yourself.

Azurite benefits the spleen, thyroid, bones, and skin. It can be carried anywhere. If chosen for jewelry, it is best worn as a ring on the right hand. Although Azurite can be used for ailments in any part of the body, it seems especially useful for the mind and mental processes. It is an integral part of many crystal- and gemstone-healing layouts. (Layouts are patterns of crystals placed on the body by crystal healers.)

Meditation can also be enhanced by Azurite, since the stone helps the mind to attain the proper mental posture that meditation requires. It then becomes easier to enter the meditative state and draw more deeply from it. Many of the goals of meditation are mirrored in the uses and abilities of Azurite.

It has an affinity with Sagittarius.

Benitoite

Benitoite is a mysterious mineral found in the American Southwest and Belgium. It can be pink, blue, purple, white, or translucent, and has a beneficial effect on the pituitary gland.

Gem literature recommends Benitoite's use as an elixir in conjunction with Neptunite and Janquinite, stating that it can amplify and improve intuition and help you be more in tune with positive ecological principles. Benitoite, Neptunite, and Janquinite working in conjunction, or as a combined elixir, can be beneficial to gardeners and botanists.

◇ ◇ ◇

Beryl

Beryl is a gemstone found in the U.S., India, and U.S.S.R. It comes in shades of yellow, gold, white, blue, or green. Both Aquamarines and Emeralds are types of Beryl.

The most basic quality of Beryl is its ability to help teach you to cease doing the unnecessary. It aids its possessor in learning how to filter out distractions and unnecessary stimulation, enabling you to pare down a stressful existence. It is good for relieving stress and for calming the mind, and is beneficial for elimination organs such as the kidneys, liver, and intestines.

Gem healers believe that Beryl will also help strengthen the circulatory and pulmonary systems, making them more resistant to toxins and pollutants. Because of its soothing properties, Beryl is supposed to be helpful to the eyes and throat and in easing a stressed mental state. Beryl is also used as a sedative, especially in conjunction with Emeralds and Lapis Lazuli.

In 1220 Arnoldus Saxo reported that the stone gave help against foes in battle, or in litigation; the wearer was rendered unconquerable and at the same time amiable, while his intellect was quickened and he was cured of laziness. In the German translation of Thomas de Cantimpre's *De Proprietatibus Rerun*, we read that Beryl reawakens the love of married people.

◇ ◇ ◇

Bloodstone

Bloodstone, commonly found in the U.S.S.R. and India, is deep green with flecks of red, often resembling drops of blood, hence its name. Technically, it is a type of opaque Quartz.

Gem literature suggests that the circulatory system is most affected by Bloodstone: it helps purify toxic blood and detoxify the kidneys, liver, and spleen. Aside from its actions as a purifying agent to the blood and related organs, Bloodstone is also said to increase courage and to help in avoiding dangerous situations by soothing the mind.

To a lesser extent, Bloodstone is said to benefit the bones, heart, and reproductive organs, all of which are blood-rich. Bloodstone is a vital, life-giving stone that stimulates courage and can also help to raise consciousness.

If Bloodstone is used for a specific healing layout, it should be used by someone who has experience with the stone.

Traditionally, the Heliotrope, or Bloodstone, was supposed to impart a reddish hue to the water in which it was placed, so that when the rays of the sun fell on the water it gave forth red reflections. From this bit of folklore the notion developed that Bloodstones had the power to turn the sun itself a blood-red, encouraging extremes of weather as a side effect.

Damigeron claimed that Bloodstone was able to announce future events by producing rain and "audible oracles," presumably high wind and thunder. Damigeron also claimed that a Bloodstone preserved the faculties and bodily health of the wearer, brought him consideration and respect, and guarded him from deception.

Bloodstone was rather extravagantly lauded in the Leyden papyrus:

> The world has no greater thing; if any one have this with him he will be given whatever he asks for; it also assuages the wrath of kings and despots, and whatever the wearer says will be believed. Whoever bears this stone, which is a gem, and pronounces the name engraved upon it, will find all doors open, while bonds and stone walls will be rent asunder.

The ancient Egyptians, in addition to using Bloodstone to assuage the wrath of kings and despots, used Bloodstone to counteract tumors and growths.

Bloodstone can be used by all signs.

Brass

Brass is a common alloy made by combining Copper and Zinc. This metal is recommended by healers as helpful to people who have unusually high levels of metal in their bloodstream, since it is a blood cleanser and detoxifier. Gem literature also suggests it for hair loss.

Bronze

Bronze is another alloy formed from Copper and Zinc. It varies little from Brass but is suggested as a character strengthener. It can also make you more aware of your goals.

Cairngorn

(See Citrine and Smoky Quartz.)

Calcite

Calcite is an abundant crystal that comes in shades of white, gray, black, green, yellow, blue, brown, or red. It is very beneficial for the cleansing organs, bones, joints, and for sharpening mental clarity.

One of the greatest benefits of using or carrying Calcite is its help in boosting your memory. It can help you draw more insight from books or personal experience by making important information easier to remember. This has a calming effect on the mind and helps you to better decide whether or not certain aspects of your life could benefit from change.

Calcite, especially green Calcite, will help you adjust to the transition from a stagnant or negative situation to a challenging, more fulfilling, and positive one. This is a good crystal for children having difficulty accepting the challenge of education. It also helps soothe the frustrations that sometimes arise from the limitations of standardized public school education.

Some athletes use Calcite because they feel it can aid the bones and joints that are stressed or injured during practice or competition.

Gold or yellow Calcite is used by people who meditate because the color is linked to the sun and light. Light is always linked with spiritual purity and knowledge. Psychics use Calcite to focus concentration. It has also been recommended for astral projection.

Gem literatures suggests that Calcite can be placed under a pyramid for a short time to amplify its abilities. Calcite is recommended for those involved in the healing professions.

◇ ◇ ◇

Carnelian

Carnelian is one of the most abundantly available and popular members of the Chalcedony family. The stone, a type of Quartz, is translucent or clear and comes in a variety of colors ranging from red to orange and, in some cases, even to dark brown.

Carnelian is very in tune with the energies of the earth and helps you to feel anchored and comfortable with your surroundings. This link with the earth also provides a connection to the past or to historical events. In a sense, Carnelian shares past experiences, paving a way for new experience.

Carnelian strongly influences the reproductive organs. The earth is often used as a symbol for fertility, and Carnelian is in tune with the earth's energy. Gem literature states that it is a good purifier for both the liver and the blood, and it is excellent for lower back trouble.

Carnelian has a stimulating nature and this can improve motivation and help you achieve greater success in career or personal matters. If a situation seems stagnant, Carnelian will help you stimulate thoughts that lead to a more challenging and enriching experience. Stated simply, it helps get you out of ruts.

Carnelian also stimulates curiosity in a

positive way, often bringing prosperity and always strengthening creativity.

If worn on the body, Carnelian lends itself best to a short pendant or a belt buckle. Many stones are carved for these purposes. Wearing Carnelian can stimulate ecological concern and appreciation.

Carnelian is grounding to people who meditate. It helps you feel settled and secure enough to want to take on greater challenges and to achieve results closer to the ideal. Carnelian is also of great value if you feel overcome by information or outside stimulation and want to clear your mind of extraneous thoughts, in order to get to the heart of the matter at hand. Whatever the situation, Carnelian allows the user to take control of his or her life and choose the direction that is most advantageous.

Wearing a Carnelian was, according to folklore, recommended to those who had a weak voice or were timid in speech. It was surmised that a warm-colored stone would give wearers the courage they lacked and allow them to speak boldly and well. (Generally, red stones were believed to have stimulating and animating effects.)

Carnelians were believed to keep away evil and deliver the wearer from the envious and from the tricks of the devil. A favorite prayer was:

In the name of God the Just, the very Just!
I implore you, O God, King of the World,

God of the World, deliver us from the
Devil
Who tries to do harm and evil to us
through
Bad people, and from the evil of the
envious.

A famous Imam, Jafar, lent the weight of
his authority to the belief in the virtue of
the Carnelian, for he declared that all the
desires of any man who wore this stone
would be gratified.

Armenians of the seventeenth century
believed that if the Carnelian was pow-
dered and taken in a potion, it would ban
all dark forebodings as well as excite joy-
ous emotions.

To Carnelian was attributed a virtue
somewhat analogous to that ascribed to
Turquoise. Anyone wearing a Carnelian
was proof against injury from falling
houses or walls. "No man who wore a Carnelian was ever found in a collapsed house
or beneath a fallen wall."

Carnelian is also mentioned in the Bible
as being used for ornamentation on breastplates for priests and soldiers.

Carnelian has affinity with Aries, Leo,
Virgo, and Capricorn.

 ◇ ◇ ◇

Cat's Eye

(See Tiger's Eye Quartz.)

◇ ◇ ◇

Chalcedony

Chalcedony is a type of Quartz that heads a family which includes Agate, Carnelian, Jasper, Tiger's Eye, and Onyx. It is found in the U.S., Sri Lanka, U.S.S.R., Mexico, and Brazil. Gray is the most common color but stones are found in shades of white, black, blue, and brown.

Chalcedony helps you to ease self-doubts and makes you more reflective. This reflection is objective and constructive, bringing on an enthusiastic perspective and open persona. It is said to ease bad dreams and problems related to the eye, gall bladder, bones, spleen, blood, and circulatory organs.

Chalcedony is cleansing in nature and will promote healing of open sores. It needn't be cleaned afterward since it has such strong cleansing qualities of its own. It absorbs and dissipates negative energy so that it can't be passed on. This makes it unique as a protector against the harsh elements and energies of the outer world.

Chalcedony also fosters the maternal instinct and is said to aid lactation.

A thirty-minute exposure to ultraviolet light or the color indigo will increase its cleansing abilities. Chalcedony is best worn as a ring, pendant, or belt buckle.

Gem literature tells us that in ancient times Chalcedony was often used in the

construction of chalices. The chalice would
be lined with silver, and this combination
protected the liquid from contamination,
insulating it from negative influences—an
important consideration in times when poi-
soning was an expedient way of disposing
of one's enemies.

An ingenious, though farfetched, explanation of the power attributed to Chalcedony of driving away "phantoms and
visions of the night" was given by Gonelli
in 1702, who claimed that the alkaline
quality of the stone dissipated the evil hu-
mors of the eye, probably removing the
diseased condition that caused the appari-
tions.

Chrysocolla

Chrysocolla is a stone that can be found in
shades of blue or green. It is mined in Mexico, Zaire, Chile, U.S.S.R., and U.S. It resembles Turquoise, and it is not surprising
that many of its properties are similar.

Arthritis and other diseases of the bones
are treated by gem healers using Chrysocolla. The organs of the digestive tract are
also aided, and ulcers become less problematic. It relieves hypertension and stressful conditions due to fear or guilt.

Chrysocolla can make you feel more
comfortable speaking the truth and helps
develop personal confidence.

Historically Chrysocolla has been used by musicians, perhaps because of its reputation for having healing properties for the throat and lungs.

Infrared light can intensify its power. Generally, a fifteen-minute exposure is sufficient.

Chrysocolla's zodiacal affinities are with Virgo and Gemini.

Chrysolite

Chrysolite is a stone found in Italy, United States, and U.S.S.R. It is most often found in shades of green or yellow, and has at times been mistaken for Topaz or Peridot.

Chrysolite energy is directly linked to the energy of the sun. It has been noted for its ability to stimulate inspiration, heighten psychic experience, and relieve negative states of mind. You may feel more personal freedom, less burdened by depression, and more receptive to spiritual matters after using Chrysolite, especially in meditation.

The appendix is said to be helped through therapy with Chrysolite, and it is employed to detoxify the cleansing organs.

Medieval literature advises those born in October:

Through Libra's sign it is quite well,
To free yourself from evil spell,

For in her gem surcease doth dwell,
The Chrysolite.

Called Topaz by the ancients, Chrysolite
was an important stone to the Egyptians,
who said that "the Serpent Isle" in the Red
Sea was guarded by watchers who freely
put to death anyone stealing unauthorized
stones. Chrysolite was mined after night-
fall, when it was revealed by its radiance:
the spot was marked and miners came
back the next day to retrieve the stones.

Pliny quotes from Juba the tradition that
Topaz (Chrysolite) derived its name from
the Island of Topazon in the Red Sea, the
first specimen having been brought by the
procurator Philemon to Berenice, mother of
Ptolemy II. According to Pliny, the mon-
arch then had a statue of his wife Arsinoe
made from the stone. Three hundred years
after Pliny, Epiphanius, clearly repeating
another version of the tale, stated that "Topaz" was set in the diadem of the "Theban
Queen."

Chrysolite set in gold is said to dispel the
terrors of the night. Its reputation for driving away evil spirits was probably due in
part to its association with the sun, before
whose life-giving rays the powers of darkness are dispelled.

Chrysoprase

Chrysoprase is a quartz stone found in the U.S.S.R., Brazil, Australia, and United States. It is a bright green crystal similar in color to green apples.

Chrysoprase helps you achieve greater personal insight, feel more calm, become less egotistical, and more open to new surroundings and situations. It will stimulate creativity and draw out unknown talents. Chrysoprase enhances fertility for both sexes and can help guard against sexually transmitted diseases.

Chrysoprase can also help gout, mental illness, and eye problems.

Swedenborg says this crystal helps one find a love of truth, while Colmar states that if a thief sentenced to be hanged or beheaded should place this stone in his mouth, he will immediately escape from his executioners. Although we are not informed in what way this fortunate result is obtained, it seems likely the stone was believed to carry the same qualities as Opal, long praised for its ability to make one invisible.

Gemini, Cancer, Aquarius, and Pisces have an affinity for Chrysoprase.

Citrine

(See Citrine Quartz.)

Copper

Copper is a plentiful metal ore that has been used for centuries both for utilitarian and decorative purposes. It ranges in color from a soft red-brown to a deep brick red. If exposed to oxygen, the surface will rust to a bright green. Copper is used today for such diverse things as cookware and computer parts. Copper is used by medical science for many ailments, particularly for inflammation.

Copper will aid in the fight against inflammatory diseases such as arthritis and rheumatism, particularly when used in conjunction with other stones. Copper helps stabilize the metabolism and heightens the actions of the cleansing organs and the immune system. The blood also benefits from Copper. Copper is beneficial for the lungs, improving the exchange of oxygen and filtering out pollutants. Soft tissue and mucous membranes retain more moisture and become less susceptible to irritation through exposure to Copper.

Copper is considered an excellent aid for increasing your ability to express and accept true feelings. Copper balances personal reserve and confidence.

Copper can be worn or carried anywhere on the body and can be made into jewelry without losing any of its effect. Those with arthritis or other inflammatory diseases may find relief if they wear Copper directly over the afflicted area.

A note of caution: Use of Copper is not suggested as a substitution for professional medical treatment but rather as a possible addition. As with other stones, it must be considered as primarily an aid to healing, not a cure.

Coral

Coral is the skeleton of sea organisms and found in oceans the world over. Almost every ancient culture used Coral for religious or health purposes. It comes in a great variety of colors and shapes. The most common colors are red, pink, white, gray, or black.

Each color of Coral has slightly different qualities. Red is stimulating, Pink is soothing, White is stabilizing, Gray is harmonizing, and Black is absorbing. Different colors of Coral can be used alone, in combination, or all together.

Because of Coral's structure and growth patterns, it is particularly sympathetic to both the skeletal structure and the circulatory system, making it a good stone for ailments of the bones and blood such as arthritis and anemia. Coral also benefits the cleansing organs and thymus, and helps battle mental illnesses.

Since Coral is an organism that builds itself up over long periods of time, it has a true link with the past and can pass knowledge along. Think of Coral as both a newborn infant open to a fascinating new world and an old sage willing to share the wisdom of experience. Edgar Cayce suggested Coral for quieting emotions.

Although aesthetic appreciation of Coral was, to primitive man, an acquired taste, the ancients believed that anyone who bore Red or White Coral could still tempests and traverse broad rivers in safety. And it was considered common knowledge that coral stanched the flow of blood from a wound, cured madness, and gave wisdom.

To have power as an amulet, though, they believed that Coral had to be used, as nearly as possible, in its natural state. In Italy, only pieces that had been freshly gathered from the sea were valued. Further, in order to exercise all its power against spells or enchantments, Coral had to be worn where its brilliant color was conspicuous. And should the Coral be accidentally broken, the magic ceased. The separate pieces had no virtue because the spirit dwelling in the Coral fled from its damaged abode, taking with it the talismanic power.

Coral is unique among healing stones because of its formation in the element of water rather than earth. In its natural state it is surrounded by, and constantly bathed in, purifying sea salt. Gem literature suggests that the healing properties of Coral can be heightened by exposure to moonlight.

Coral is also unusual in that it has a zodiacal affinity with all signs. Coral is recommended for artists, athletes, chiropractors, lecturers, dentists, farmers, and osteopaths.

◊ ◊ ◊

Creedite

Creedite is a white stone found in the United States and Mexico. It is beneficial to the body's cleansing system and is useful for blood detoxification. Creedite helps you discover how best to express yourself and how to intuitively understand other people. Creedite will also benefit the nervous system by aiding in the transmission of nerve impulses.

◊ ◊ ◊

Cuprite

Cuprite is a red to brown mineral found in the United States, Australia, Mexico, and U.S.S.R. It is beneficial for the metabolical imbalances many people experience. Cuprite helps the heart and blood, muscle tissue, and skeletal system.

Gem literature suggests cuprite for people having difficulty dealing with father or authority figures. It is also considered helpful in investigating past-life experiences.

◇ ◇ ◇

Diamond

Diamonds are considered by some to be the purest expression of gemstones the earth has ever produced. Their clarity and ability to refract the entire light spectrum is peerless in the gem world. They will phosphoresce when exposed to radium, polonium, or actinum. They are without question the hardest substance produced by nature.

Diamonds are composed of pure carbon and are formed by thousands of years of intense heat and pressure. Because of their hardness and purity, they are much in demand for industrial uses as well as for jewelry and gemstone healing. They are a symbol of wealth and power and have been highly coveted for centuries. Diamonds and roses are often considered the only two things from nature that have reached their evolutionary pinnacles.

When considering the use of a Diamond for healing purposes, one must ignore its monetary value and concentrate upon the stone's unique relationship with energy. Because of its ability to amplify the energy of whatever it comes in contact with, a Diamond is frequently combined with other gems or crystals. If used, for example, with Aquamarine, a Diamond will increase the cleansing properties and mental soothing that Aquamarine helps to produce. If worn or carried alone, a Diamond will amplify the energy of the wearer. Unfortunately, this includes any negative energy the wearer might possess as well. But if the wearer has positive energy, he or she will experience amplification that can lead to the realization of the purity of white light.

White light is the perfect balance of all color. It is an ideal state in which all the components work together to produce energy in its purest state. Consequently, if you have a positive attitude, you can learn from Diamonds and balance and blend all the aspects of your own life into a pure and cohesive entity that, in turn, amplifies the energy state surrounding you.

Some gem literature contends that the blue light within the color spectrum of a Diamond is beneficial for glaucoma. This is because of Diamond's ability to refract all colors without diluting or filtering them. It has also been suggested that Diamonds are beneficial to the brain and testicles. If worn, Diamonds are recommended for the earlobes.

Folklore about Diamonds is conflicting. They were said to be an antidote for poisons, and yet the stone itself was thought to be a deadly poison. Further, the Italian physician Gonelli claimed the diamond grew dark in the presence of poison.

A Diamond was also believed to afford protection from plague or pestilence, proof of its powers being that plague attacked the poorer classes and spared the rich, who could afford to deck themselves out with the stones.

The *Lapidario* of Alfonso X recommends Diamonds for diseases of the bladder but only in desperate cases.

Marbodus suggested Diamonds were a cure for insanity while Hinus warned that it was dangerous to use diamonds of inferior quality for curative purposes—not only were they unlikely to cure the disease, but they might cause lameness, jaundice, pleurisy, or even leprosy as a side effect. Diamonds of good quality were to be used only after a seven-day purification in cow urine, and then only judiciously.

In all cases, however, the stone had to touch the skin to be effective, and, according to widespread superstition, the talismanic power of a Diamond was ruined if it were acquired by purchase; it could only be received as a gift. (The spirit dwelling in the stone was thought to be offended at being bought and sold.)

Traditionally, a Diamond was the emblem of fearlessness and invincibility, the male equivalent to the Pearl. Diamonds were thought to bring victory to the wearer by endowing him with superior strength, fortitude, and courage. Marbodus tells us it is a stone of great power in driving away nocturnal specters and, to this purpose, should be worn in gold on the left arm. St. Hildegard claimed a Diamond was a great enemy of the Devil because it resisted His power day and night.

Cardano, however, has this to say of Diamonds: "It is believed to make the wearer unhappy; its effects therefore are the same upon the mind as that of the sun upon the eye, for the latter rather dims than strengthens the sight. It indeed engenders fearlessness, but there is nothing that contributes more to our safety than prudence and fear; therefore it is better to fear."

Once associated with lightning, the diamond was also believed to owe its origin to the thunderbolt. Alternatively, it is sometimes claimed to be consumed or melted by thunder (not illogically, assuming that the same force that was supposed to have formed the stone should be able to dissolve it). That the diamond can be entirely consumed at a high temperature was a fact not known in Europe in the fourteenth century.

The Arabians and Persians, as well as modern Egyptians, agree in attributing to the diamond a wonderful power to bring good fortune. Rabbi Benoni (a fourteenth century mystic) asserted that it produced somnambulism and, as a talisman, so powerfully attracted the planetary influences that it rendered the wearer invincible. It was also said to provoke a state of spiritual ecstasy.

An alchemist of the same century, Pierre

de Boniface, asserted that a Diamond made the wearer invisible.

With all of its other attributes, it is not surprising that sexual and reproductive powers were associated with Diamonds. Sir John Mandeville wrote, "I have often times tried the experiment that if a man keep them with a little of the rock, and water them with May dew often, they shall grow every year and the small will grow great." Whether or not Diamonds will reproduce if thus encouraged is in question, but it is understandable that Diamonds are still used in engagement rings today: they are said to enhance the love of a husband for his wife.

Emeralds and Amethyst Quartz are especially amplified by Diamonds.

Diamond has a zodiacal affinity with all signs and is the commonly assigned birthstone of those born in April.

◇ ◇ ◇

Emerald

Esoteric literature has stated that an Emerald was brought to earth by the Lords of Flame from the planet Venus. Despite its unauthenticated origin, Emerald is an important stone to anyone who works in science or healing. It provides inspiration and helps those in need of balance, healing, and infinite patience.

Emerald comes from the Beryl family (which also brings us Aquamarine), and is found in shades of green varying from very light to very deep.

An Emerald helps the wearer gain physical, emotional, and mental equilibrium. An inspirational and relaxing stone, it can be worn by anyone without ill effects. The pale, clear, green Emeralds are valuable in meditative work as well as healing.

Although an Emerald is often combined with other stones in pieces of jewelry, it works best when combined with a Diamond or worn alone. It is one of the few gemstones that can be deeply flawed and still retain its value in the eyes of gem lovers.

An Emerald gives wisdom from the mental plane, so that the possessor is motivated to give love and wisdom to others. Some gemstone books suggest that Emeralds help strengthen the backbone and alleviate problems associated with sugar diabetes.

Wear an Emerald on the little finger or ring finger. It can also be worn as a pendant over the heart center (in the middle of the chest) or as a bracelet on the right arm. Do not wear an Emerald constantly. It should only be worn when the wearer feels the need to have it near.

Man-made specimens are helpful, though not as beneficial as natural Emeralds. The body has more difficulty assimilating the energy of a man-made stone. Man-made stones do not contain all the elements present in natural stones.

The force field of this stone is different in

its virgin state than when it is faceted to reflect light. There is one exception, the opaque variety (which should not be used for mental or emotional attunement).

A carved design on the surface of an Emerald sends out points of energy into a particular area of reference that differs according to the inscribed symbol. It will manifest the essence of the symbol on the ethers and emit its essences and contribution. Clear greens are valuable for meditation.

Emeralds are of special value to athletes, chiropractors, lecturers, marriage counselors, masseurs, optometrists, people who work in radioactive areas, and those who work in close quarters.

An Emerald improves psychic abilities, raises consciousness, and helps the individual attain balance. It also enhances the immune system.

Emeralds were believed to foreshadow future events, but we do not know whether visions were actually seen in the stone, as they were in spheres of rock crystal or Beryl, or an Emerald endowed the wearer with a supernatural foreknowledge of things to come. As an enemy of all enchantments and conjurations, Emeralds were feared by magicians, who found all their arts of no avail if an Emerald were in their vicinity.

Emeralds were used to strengthen memory, to aid in eloquence, and to reveal the truth or falsity of a lover's oaths (although regarded as an enemy of sexual passion).

Light-colored Emeralds were considered the best because they were reputed to be "brought from the nest of griffons."

Emeralds were employed as antidotes for poisons and poisoned wounds, as well as against demonical possession. Worn about the neck, they were said to cure epilepsy.

In the third century, the precious stone mentioned by Theophrastus in his treatise on gems was an Emerald, the use of which was suggested to relieve eyestrain. So prevalent was this theory through time that gem engravers kept Emeralds on their worktables so as to be able to look at the stone from time to time to relieve eyestrain.

In the thirteenth century Hindu physicians considered an Emerald to be an effective laxative. It also cured dysentery, diminished the secretion of bile, and stimulated the appetite, promoting bodily health and destroying demonical influences.

Teifashi (1242 A.D.) believed an Emerald was a cure for haemoptysis and dysentery if worn over the liver of the person affected. To cure gastric troubles it was to be laid upon the stomach. Wherever Emeralds were kept, the wearer was protected from the attacks of venomous creatures, and evil spirits were driven away. Perhaps the light reflected from many of these gems suggested the idea that they radiated a certain curative energy. It was also believed that a serpent could not look on an Emerald without losing its sight.

A certain cure for dysentery in the 1600s, was to wear an Emerald suspended so that it touched the abdomen. Another Emerald was then placed in the mouth.

Emeralds have an affinity with Cancer, Taurus, and Libra, and the deeper, clearer stones attune well to Taurus and Scorpio.

Enstatite/Diopside

Enstatite is a brown, green, or white stone found in Japan, Germany, Ireland, and the United States. Diopside is found in similar colors and is mined in the U.S.S.R. and India in addition to the countries already mentioned. These stones are mentioned together because they have identical properties.

Both benefit the circulatory system and cleansing organs. Mental clarity results from healing layouts that include Enstatite and/or Diopside. Diopside is recommended for public speakers, students, and surgeons.

Flint

Flint is a gray, white, black, red, or brown stone found in all countries around the world. It is beneficial to the entire body. All tissue, internal or external, will be helped, but especially the cardiopulmonary and cleansing systems. Use Flint to feel more whole and healthy. It can give a strong boost to your mental state and as such is extremely helpful for persons who have been afflicted by degenerative diseases.

Fluorite

Fluorite is familiar to us because of its association with fluoride, the common tooth-decay preventative that is added to toothpaste and in some areas to community drinking water. The crystals are usually translucent and come in shades of white, brown, blue, yellow, purple, red, or are colorless.

Fluorite, like fluoride, benefits the teeth and bones. In some ancient civilizations it was used as a cure for cancerous growths.

People with arthritis, rheumatism, or spinal injuries have reported some relief from their conditions when they employ Fluorite in their healing regimen. It can help to rekindle sexual appetite and heighten intuitive powers.

Gem literature suggests using Fluorite in conjunction with Calcite and Pyrite.

Fluorite aids in fighting mental disorder and gaining spiritual awakening. It can help make you more aware of the higher levels of reality and can anchor and free you from over-stimulation on the psychic plane. Green Fluorite is a valuable helper in grounding excess energies.

Fluorite is best worn on the earlobes. It is a young gem, still evolving into its full acceptance by mankind.

It has an affinity with Pisces.

Garnet

Garnets range in color from deep emerald green through yellow, brown, and red. We are most familiar with the red translucent Pyrope and Rhodolite Garnets that are common to the United States, but Garnets are found all over the world.

Many of the Garnets sold in gem stores are uncut and vary from pea size to stones with the diameter of a golf ball. They stimulate creativity, passion, and the circulatory system.

When used in conjunction with the pituitary gland, Garnets help to provide past-life information. They should be placed on the center of the forehead. If carried around in the pocket and then placed on the forehead of another person, closer ties will form with that individual.

Green Garnets are healing stones. Red Garnets represent love and help the aspirant to strive for improvement in moral conduct. Square-cut Garnets help bring about business opportunities and filter out concerns that are not one's own; rectangular shapes aid in matters of intellect or the earth. Garnets teach patience and constancy and are not to be used lightly. They develop love and compassion.

Red has long been considered the color of passion and is obviously the color of blood. Red Garnets can also help you tune into the energy of the heart and take control of your sexuality. They can rekindle feelings and renew love, helping you express emotions with greater ease. Garnets sharpen self-perception and extend that openness to others. They also help to calm anger, particularly anger directed towards the self.

Best worn at the earlobes or as a pendant over the heart, Garnets have the greatest affinity with Aquarius, Leo, Aries, Scorpio, and Capricorn. As birthstones they are appropriate for those born in January.

Gold

For centuries gold has been coveted not only for its monetary value but for its amazing purity. No other metal achieves such astonishing flexibility in both its pure and alloyed states. Modern medical science uses gold for numerous reconstructive purposes as well as a remedy for many diseases such as arthritis. Gold is also used extensively for industrial purposes because of its ability to conduct energy and transmit information without distortion. The only metal virtually impervious to the elements, it never tarnishes. As the softest metal, it is usually alloyed to give it strength.

Because of its amazing conductive ability, Gold is well suited to healing. Gold is a regenerator, helping one renew oneself. It works on the physical, mental, and spiritual planes. Extreme situations in any of these areas can be better balanced with Gold.

Literature suggests that Gold benefits the nervous system and improves the ability of the nerves to transmit information in the most efficient manner. It helps digestion and aids the body in the proper assimilation of food. The circulatory system and blood will benefit from Gold, which serves to detoxify the blood. Hormonal and chemical imbalances can be better controlled since all glands that determine the levels of these substances will work with greater efficiency. Gold can be of great importance to individuals with degenerative diseases, such as heart disease or arthritis, because it helps rid the body of blockages.

Gold helps you find ways to better control emotional extremes or deal better with stressful situations. Gold increases the ability of the body to exchange oxygen from the lungs to the blood, thereby helping the brain work more efficiently. An amplifier of impressive strength, it sharpens focus on issues that will have the most positive effect and improve your quality of life. It will assist the user in the search for satisfaction and meaning, helping to filter out unnecessary distractions or to interpret situations with a more objective attitude. It helps you view yourself realistically.

If you are timid or feel defeated, Gold will boost confidence and help to amplify the qualities that make you an important and valuable person. Gold strengthens the appreciation of positive qualities in others. Because the production of neurotransmitters is stepped up, all functions of the brain are balanced and improved. Gold helps you use both sides of the brain with greater ease, balancing creativity and intuition with practicality. In its purest state, Gold is the greatest conductor of its kind. With a little altering it still transmits well.

Gold works well with all crystals and gemstones. It can be used in conjunction with Copper and Silver, which aid in boosting its abilities in specific instances.

Granite

Granite is a common rock found worldwide. It is widely accepted as a building material but also has healing properties. It comes in shades of pink, green, gray, yellow, and white.

This stone benefits the bones and muscle

and soft tissue. Gem experts suggest using this stone in conjunction with Flint to stimulate the regeneration of the body's tissue.

◊ ◊ ◊

Hematite

Hematite is an iron oxide, steel gray to iron black in color. Sometimes it has deep red spots on the surface. It is found in the United States, Brazil, and Canada.

The iron in this mineral has a strong effect on the blood and gemstone literature stresses its use in supporting the kidney's blood-cleansing function. Hematite is a protective stone and helps bolster low self-esteem. It is said to aid tissue regeneration. It is also used for astral projection.

Hematite was used by Galen for inflamed eyelids and headaches, and by Pliny for blood disorders. Egyptians valued it as a cure for hysteria. Azchalias asserted that Hematite, when used as a talisman, procured for the wearer a favorable hearing of petitions addressed to kings and a fortunate issue of lawsuits and judgments. Because of its association with Mars, it was also considered to be of invaluable help to warriors rubbing their bodies with it. Perhaps, like the lodestone, it was believed to confer invulnerability.

If worn, Hematite should be placed at the base of the spine.

Herkimer Diamond

(See Quartz.)

Hiddenite

Hiddenite is a green gemstone, a form of spodumene found in North Carolina. It is beneficial for the cleansing and digestive systems.

Indocolite

(See Blue Tourmaline.)

Ivory

Ivory is generally considered to be the bone of mammals, and most Ivory comes from elephants, walruses, or whales. Unfortunately, these animals are hunted and killed for this rare material. There are organizations working to protect these animals and laws on the books against hunting them, but poachers have killed so many that certain species are on the brink of extinction.

Because of this, use Ivory only if you are very drawn to it. Ivory can be found mostly in white or cream, although some shades of pink and yellow do exist.

Because of Ivory's connection to teeth, it is especially well suited for ailments of the bones, joints, and teeth. The skin will benefit from it, as will the circulatory system because of Ivory's ability to boost the body's ability to detoxify.

Ivory affects the way you examine your own existence and helps you become more introspective and analytical. Beneficial side effects of this could be greater insights into your expectations and an understanding of how to make them more realistic and attainable. Ivory may make you more in tune with animals and nature, but you have to have this desire in order to open a path for this expression.

For centuries Ivory has been used in jewelry that can be worn all over the body. Much of the time it is worn as a fetish or for ritual purposes.

When considering Ivory for yourself, you must always consider why it is important to possess it. If its spiritual value is great enough, you can proceed with the purchase and simply wrestle with the ecological ramifications (it would perhaps help to make a spiritual offering to the animal who died). But if Ivory is only perceived as jewelry that has nice side effects or as an object of great monetary value, then it would seem wisest to forget it.

Jade

Jade is a peaceful stone that has for centuries been of primary importance to the people of the Orient, where it is considered one of the most important symbols of purity and serenity. A highly prized stone, it is used for intricately carved, ornate sculptures and jewelry. Often mentioned in Chinese and Japanese folklore and religious parables, Jade was a primary element used in adorning the persons of royalty and religious leaders as well as their castles and temples. It was a high honor to be able to possess Jade for its spiritual value as well as its obvious beauty.

There are two varieties of Jade, Jadeite and Nephrite. Of these, Jadeite has always been more coveted and sought after. Nephrite is quite similar to Jadeite in its healing abilities, but its colors are creamier and less translucent than Jadeite; Nephrite is the more commonly found variety.

Jade comes in a wide range of colors that include white, lavender, red, brown, yellow, orange, blue, and green. While all Jade has some healing influence, each color relates more specifically to certain ailments or organs.

Properties common to all colors of Jade include its ability to mellow one's existence. It helps you to rid yourself of negative thoughts and energy, since it soothes the mind and makes tasks seem easier and less complicated. It strengthens the body's filtration and cleansing systems and assists in the removal of toxins. Jade is very beneficial to the heart in both physical and spiritual senses. Anyone can develop a greater capacity for love by utilizing Jade properly, since Jade gives its energy to whomever it comes in contact with. Jade never asks for anything in return for sharing its abilities; it simply offers them in goodwill, a powerful lesson.

Jade is also a very protective stone and will keep its wearer out of harm's way.

Such is the fondness of the Chinese for Jade that those who can afford the luxury of it carry small pieces with them so that they always have it in hand. They believe that, when handled, some of the secret virtue of the substance is absorbed into the body.

When struck, Jade emits a peculiarly melodious sound that for the Chinese has come to resemble the voice of a loved one. Jade is termed the concentrated essence of love.

Jade amulets are worn by children to protect them from the danger of childhood diseases.

Egyptians, Mexicans, and Chinese all put small pieces of Jade into the mouths of the deceased.

The name Jade is derived from the Spanish term *piedra de hijada*, meaning literally "stone of the flank," which is said to have been derived from the Indian use of it as a curative for kidney disease. In ancient times Jade appears to have been looked upon as a great aid to women giving birth, and many ingenious conjectures have been advanced as to the connection between this belief and the form of some of the prehistoric objects made of this material.

Sir Walter Raleigh said of Jade:

> These Amazones have likewise great store of these plates of gold, which they recover by exchange, chiefly for a kind of greene stone, which the Spaniards call Piedras Hijadas, and we use for spleene stones and for the disease of the stone we also esteeme them. Of these I saw divers in Guiana, and commonly every King or Casique had one, which theire wives for the most part weare, and they esteeme them as great jewels.

By the middle of the seventeenth century the curative power of Jade for various forms of kidney and bladder stones was generally accepted. A singular instance is offered in one of Voiture's letters upon receiving a beautiful Jade bracelet from Mademoiselle Paulet. She was apparently a fellow sufferer of kidney stones and, in seeking to relieve his pain, compromised her virtue when Voiture's friends mistook it as a gift of love.

All signs of the zodiac will benefit from Jade.

Blue Jade

Blue Jade is a peaceful and passive energy source. The color blue is symbolic of peace, heaven, and reflection. People who meditate can use Blue Jade to relax and gain an inner serenity that will help them in their quest for simple knowledge. It is a quiet teacher of patience and slow, steady progress. Blue Jade is a wonderful stone to give to people who feel restricted or overcome by situations beyond their control.

Brown Jade

Brown Jade is a stone that connects us to the earth. Its earthy color is comforting, its energy steady and reliable. It is a good stone to use to help settle matters of the home or to adjust to a new environment. Brown Jade is used extensively in statuary and ornamentation.

Green Jade

Green Jade is the most common and popular color available. It has all the general Jade qualities already mentioned and is very calming to the nervous system. The color green is representative of life or growth. Green Jade helps you channel passions in a constructive way, making expressions of love easier.

Lavender Jade

Lavender Jade is in touch with the emotions, and is beneficial to people who have been hurt by love or need to discover the gentleness within themselves. This stone can help you learn restraint and subtlety in matters of emotional importance.

Red Jade

Red Jade is a passionate and active stone. Red has been associated with many things, among them love, anger, and madness. Not surprisingly, Red Jade does have some connection to all of these. It can have such a stimulating influence that the wearer becomes agitated and feels the need to express anger. As frightening as this may seem, no matter how happy or positive you are, everyone has some angry feelings, and Red Jade can help to extract these feelings and teach you to come to terms with them. Delusion and madness can be the result of pent-up anger and other emotions that fester and pollute a person mentally and spiritually. Use Red Jade to blow off steam, to release tension. It can provide an opportunity to identify and rid yourself of something that, if ignored for too long, will grow and become unmanageable.

White or Cream Jade

White or Cream-colored Jade will help you direct your energy to its most advantageous outlet. It helps to filter out distraction and allows you to envision the best result of a given situation. Decisions become easier to make and are based more on pertinent information than on unrelated complications. Some gem healers also suggest White Jade for the eyes.

Yellow and Orange Jade

Yellow and Orange Jade are similar enough to be considered together. Both colors are stimulating and energetic, but the warmth of both also adds a mellowness that is more soothing than frenetic. They are both in tune with the energy of the sun and impart the gift of joy and happiness. Both colors teach the interconnectedness of all beings. They help organs that process food and waste in our bodies. In a proper ecological cycle, each order of life feeds or lives off another order, creating a balance that ensures everyone will survive. These stones help you assume a conscientious role in that cycle.

Jasper

Jasper is another member of the Chalcedony family. Found worldwide, it comes in shades of red, yellow, green, or brown.

Many experts of gemstone healing suggest using this tone for elixirs because it will not over-stimulate any part of the body. (See the Glossary to find out more about elixirs.) In fact, this stone is considered more effective if it is used for long periods of time because it works slowly. Any benefit derived from Jasper takes time to accomplish because it is a methodical and meticulous worker. But the overall result of prolonged use of Jasper in healing practices will be a unifying of all aspects of your life. With patience anyone using Jasper will feel a continuity of spirit and body that can vastly improve both work and play. In addition, each color of Jasper has additional specific qualities when used alone.

Jasper had great repute in ancient times as a rain bringer. The fourth-century author of *Lithica* states:

> The gods propitious hearken to his
>   prayers,
> who'ever the polished glass-green
>   Jasper wears:
> His parched glebe they'll satiate with
>   rain,
> And send for showers to soak the
>   thirsty plain.

Perhaps the green hue of this stone suggested its association with green fields.

In the fourth century Jasper was reputed to drive away evil spirits and protect those who wore it from the bites of venomous creatures. An anonymous German author of the eleventh or twelfth century claimed that if Jasper is placed on a snakebite, the venom would be drawn from the wound.

Jasper was set in gold and used as a stone in the breastplates of the high priests in the time of Aaron.

Gem literature suggests that Jasper works well in conjunction with Opals.

Jasper is recommended for executives as an aid to quick thinking. It will also help them endure stress.

Brown Jasper

Brown Jasper is also known as Picture Jasper. As with many stones that are brown, it is connected to the energies of the earth and helps you find stability and balance. It can benefit ailments that result from environmental pollution. Brown Jasper is said to boost the immune system and assist in extracting pollutants and toxins from the body. Keep in mind that this process takes some time since Jaspers work slowly. Jasper will also add to the ability of the cleansing system and its related organs, and will improve the skin (toxins and pollutants are a major cause of eruptions and irritation to the skin).

Brown Jasper can help you become more ecologically aware. It influences decisions that could positively affect the level to which you allow yourself to add pollution to the environment, particularly diesel fuel and cigarette smoke.

Stones that are in tune with earth energy retain strong memories of the past. Brown

Jasper is well suited for use by people who wish to relive past events through regression or analysis. The greatest benefit from this activity comes from the fact that past-life experiences can at times prove to be hidden stumbling blocks for present and future activities. Through analysis of these blocking events, you can overcome them and progress.

Green Jasper

Green Jasper is especially suited to tempering aspects of your life that have taken on too great an importance. If you are expending great amounts of energy trying to improve one part of yourself, you may tend to ignore other parts, creating an imbalance. Certain individuals may even reach a point where this personal imbalance causes a collapse of their everyday ability to function. Green Jasper counters this by working as a gentle daily reminder that the whole is only the result of all the parts.

Green Jasper works best on ailments of the upper torso, digestive tract, and the cleansing organs.

Red Jasper

Red Jasper is much like Bloodstone in its link to the circulatory system. Some say it is beneficial in battling diseases of the blood and detoxifying blood-rich organs like the liver. Its stimulating energy can bring problems to light before they are a threat.

Yellow Jasper

Yellow Jasper is beneficial to the endocrine glands and the cleansing organs. This is an energizing stone that makes you feel stronger and in better physical condition. Positive energy and thoughts can have a dramatic effect on actual physical condition, and Yellow Jasper is a great means of channeling that positive energy.

Jet

Jet is another example of fossilized organic matter that has been used for centuries as a healing stone. (It was used by both the Greeks and Romans.) Jet is a form of petrified wood similar to coal, though it is much harder. When people describe things as jet black, they are referring to this stone. Black has long been known for its absorbing qualities, and this applies to Jet as well. In ancient times it was used to ease everything from colds, fever, and menstrual cramps to swelling and mental disorders.

When using Jet, keep in mind its absorbing nature. It will help to draw out negative energy. This is especially useful for people who have unreasonable fears that limit their lives. Jet can help you achieve more control of your life by helping to control mood swings and fighting deep depression. Some gem healers recommend it for stimulating psychic experience and guiding one in the quest for spiritual enlightenment.

If worn, Jet should be set in silver.

Jet has been found among the paleolithic remains in the caves of the Kesslerlock in Switzerland. Quite possibly Jet, as well as Amber, was already regarded as possessing a certain talismanic virtue. When worn, ornaments made from these stones were believed to become a part of the very body and soul of the wearer and therefore were regarded with jealous care. Necklaces, bracelets, and rings were favored as ways in which to position talismanic gems next to the skin.

Jet was also used as amulets by the Pueblos.

◊ ◊ ◊

Kunzite

Kunzite is a pink stone that has a high mineral content of lithium. This mineral has been used extensively by the medical profession for psychiatric disorders. Its color relates it to the energy of the circulatory system, especially the blood, and the lungs will also benefit from exposure to Kunzite. It is a soothing stone that can help you adjust to the pressures of modern life.

Kunzite has an affinity with Taurus and Libra.

Labradorite

Labradorite is a blue feldspar often used in ornaments and decoration. Gem literature sometimes refers to it as Spectrolite. Gem healers claim it elevates the wearer's consciousness and connection with the energies of the universe.

It has affinities with Aquarius, Pisces, Sagittarius, and Capricorn.

◇ ◇ ◇

Lapis Lazuli WEAR AS CLOSE TO THROA AS POSSIBLE

Lapis Lazuli is an extraordinarily deep blue stone often flecked with Pyrite. Lapis stones can also be mottled with white Calcite. Most of the world's Lapis Lazuli is currently mined in the U.S.S.R. and Afghanistan.

Lapis Lazuli has been used for centuries for both spiritual and decorative purposes. Perhaps the best known examples lie in the artifacts from the ancient civilization of Egypt.

Lapis Lazuli can be beneficial to the respiratory system, especially the throat and lungs, the cleansing organs, and the nervous system. It is considered a good stone for blood purification and for boosting the immune system.

Lapis Lazuli's greatest single attribute is

its relationship to the mind and the mental state. It is a powerful thought-amplifier and is helpful in aligning all the elements of the body and mind. It can increase psychic abilities and will open the third eye.

Blue is a color often related to water, peace, spiritual attainment, and serenity. All these relate to Lapis Lazuli. It is a stone that can guide you in the direction of mental and spiritual purity.

Within everyone lies an essence comprised of physical, mental, and spiritual energies. Many things in this world distract us from devoting time to harmonizing these energies. If we are distracted for too long, our lives may go out of balance. Illness, depression, or doubts about the purpose of existence can be serious side effects of this imbalance. With Lapis Lazuli as a friend and guide, we can become more in touch with our essence and play a more active role in the control of our existence. Lapis is used by many people to broaden their knowledge of themselves and their environment.

Lapis is one of the greatest stones for attaining enlightenment and as such should be used with great caution and care. Wear it as close to the throat as possible. Although it has traditionally been used as a ring, it should be worn above the diaphragm so that the energy of the wearer is drawn upward.

Lapis Lazuli has a great deal of raw power but is only as good as the person who wears it. In short, it brings forth the power inherent in an individual. It is an enhancer and a leveling force.

Lapis Lazuli was highly valued in ancient Babylon and Egypt. In the Middle Ages, Albertus Magnus stated it was a cure for melancholy and for the "quartern fever" (apparently an intermittent fever that returned every third day).

Named Chesbet by the Egyptians, a quantity of Lapis often appeared as an important item in the list of tribute paid to Egypt by those countries under her influence. It was often listed among the gifts sent by Babylonia. This Babylonian Lapis was from the oldest mines in the world, which were being worked in 4000 B.C. and are still being worked to this day.

The Egyptian high priest is said to have worn, suspended from his neck, an image of Mat, goddess of truth, made of Lapis Lazuli.

Lapis Lazuli was also valued because of its extraordinarily beautiful blue color, which was retained even when the stone was ground up and mixed with pigment. In this form it was used for centuries as an expensive and luxurious makeup as well as a paint for only the finest artists.

Lapis Lazuli was another of the stones set in the breastplates of the high priests of Israel.

Lapis Lazuli has affinity with Taurus, Aquarius, and Sagittarius.

Lazulite

Lazulite is a blue or green stone mined in the United States, Brazil, and Afghanistan. It has calming effects upon the mind and helps the body filter out toxins. Lazulite can boost the immune system and improve the purity of the blood.

Lazulite primarily helps you organize your life. It can facilitate more cohesive thought patterns and help you feel greater confidence in yourself and your role in the world. It is also recommended for blocked creative energies.

Gem literature suggests that this stone be worn on the right middle finger.

This is a good stone for people working in communication or creative fields.

Limestone

Limestone is a plentiful mineral found worldwide. It comes in a great variety of colors, including black, white, brown, red, yellow, and green. Limestone is reputed as a detoxifier of the body and brain. It rids one of blockages of all kinds.

Gem literature suggests Limestone for creative individuals or those struck by sudden fears.

Magnetite

Magnetite is a dark brown or gray stone that is magnetic. It is an iron-based lodestone found in India, Mexico, and United States. It has beneficial effects upon the blood and circulatory system.

When considering its uses, keep in mind Magnetite's positive and negative charges and how these charges work together. You can use the stone's power to attract and to repel, to energize and de-energize.

In Chinese medicine, if a body organ is diseased it has excess "heat," which means it is over-stimulated, or the body is working too hard to heal itself. Magnetite can help stimulate a sluggish organ with attractive magnetism or calm an over-active one with repellent magnetism.

In recent years the use of magnetic therapy has met with positive results in England and Japan. As with any new technique or technology, there is some controversy regarding its actual benefits. However, Magnetite is being used extensively for sports injuries and asthma with positive results. Magnetite may prove to be a stone that medical science turns to for healing in the near future.

Magnetite was known in ancient times as a lodestone. According to Plato, its more usual name was "the Heraclean stone."

Pliny states, on the authority of Nicander, that a certain Magnes, a shepherd, discovered the mineral on Mount Ida while pasturing his flock, because the nails of his shoes clung to a piece of it. We are also told by Pliny that Ptolemy, planning to erect a temple in honor of his sister and wife, called in the aid of Chirocrates, an Alexandrian architect. The latter was engaged to construct an iron statue of the woman that should appear to hang in midair without support. Unfortunately, the king and his architect died before the design could be realized.

In the fourth century it was believed that a piece of lodestone, if placed beneath the pillow of a sleeping wife, would act as a touchstone of her virtue. And Alexander the Great provided his soldiers with lodestones as a defense against the wily activity of jinns, or evil spirits. Lodestone, along with ordinary magnetized iron, was regarded as a sure defense against enchantments.

In July 1887 a woman in Macon, Georgia, sued a conjuror to recover five dollars that she had paid for a piece of lodestone to serve as a charm to bring back her wandering husband. Since the market value of this mineral was only 75 cents a pound and the piece small, the judge ordered the money refunded.

Malachite

Usually found in association with Azurite, Malachite is a stone with a color range from light to dark green. It is often variegated and is one of the basic ores of Copper.

<u>Malachite should be used with extreme care because it can amplify negative qualities</u>. Caution must always be used when wearing it as jewelry. However, Malachite also magnifies the positive, and so it is useful if your mood is definitely on the upswing. The safest way to wear this stone is in a polished ring on the left hand.

Malachite should not be used in healing without careful consideration of who is doing the healing. Some gem literature claims that Malachite is still evolving and is in the state of becoming a master key to future healing and balancing techniques. Malachite is useful for relaxation and neurological disorders as well as tissue regeneration.

Malachite's green color is strongly in tune with nature, the force of life, and healing. It has an affinity with earth and water. It is also said to awaken healing qualities. It is useful in fighting mental illnesses. It also is said to stimulate the optic nerve, to help the pancreas, spleen, parathyroid, and to help dyslexia. To the Rosicrucians, Malachite symbolizes the rising of the spiritual man. It will assist with visions of all kinds.

People living near nuclear power plants should keep pieces of Malachite in their homes, since Malachite may expel plutonium. A warning: Malachite dust particles are highly toxic and their ingestion should be avoided.

The Egyptians used Malachite for protection and safeguarding pregnancy. The stones were ground up and used as an eye remedy as well as a cosmetic.

In Italy, Malachite was used to protect against the evil eye.

Malachite was also considered a talisman particularly appropriate for children. If a piece of this stone were attached to an infant's cradle, all evil spirits were held at bay, enabling the child to sleep soundly and peacefully.

In some parts of Germany, Malachite shared with Turquoise the reputation of protecting the wearer from danger in falling. It was said to warn of coming danger by breaking into pieces.

The stone has an affinity with Scorpio.

Malachite/Azurite

This is a natural blending of two beneficial stones that in combination produce a synergistic relationship. It is a blue-green stone that is helpful to anyone. Malachite has the ability to draw out positive or negative energy, and Azurite is soothing and calming to the spirit. Together they have the ability to neutralize energy and produce a sense of calm. This is cleansing in nature and can positively affect the psyche because Malachite/Azurite detoxifies the spirit. Sleep will improve and you will be better able to interpret your dreams.

All signs of the zodiac will benefit from this stone.

◇ ◇ ◇

Marble

Marble is another common and plentiful stone that is generally found in the United States, Italy, and Greece. It comes in shades of white, brown, yellow, red, green, gray, and black.

Marble is a cleansing stone that is beneficial for the blood, skin, and cleansing systems.

◇ ◇ ◇

Meteorite

Meteorites are rocks of varying size that fall to Earth from places of unknown origin in space. Oftentimes, Meteorites are called shooting stars because as they descend through the Earth's atmosphere they leave a trail of burning matter behind them. Owing to their mysterious origins they are interpreted by many people in terms of their ability to affect change in one's life.

Some people reason that Meteorites are in tune with the energies of the cosmos and therefore more capable of raising our energies to a universal level. Others speculate that since they have no connection to Earth, Meteorites can in no way influence our lives.

Perhaps a reasonable way to approach this stone is to try and tune into its energy on an intuitive level and decide whether or not it would play a good role in your life. This is a good rule for all stones or gems of the Earth as well. If you feel drawn to or compelled to own a particular stone, you should follow intuition.

◊ ◊ ◊

Moonstone

Moonstones are translucent, milky gemstones usually pale blue or green that are cut from Albite. They are found in India and Australia and are known to be of ancient spiritual significance in their connection to the moon and the intuitive aspect of one's nature.

Moonstones help cool, soothe, and calm over-reactions to emotional and personal situations as well as make us conscious of the fact that all things are part of a cycle of constant change. Moonstones open us up to the feminine and are associated with sensitivity, intuition, and clairvoyance. This can be very helpful for men with excessive macho problems.

Farmers have long used the cycles of the moon as a gauge for the best times to plant crops. This makes Moonstone beneficial for individuals involved in agriculture.

Moonstone's effect upon the menstrual cycle is powerful. At the time of the full moon or menstruation, women should be aware of their sensitive emotional nature and remove these stones. Moonstone may help all parts of the lower torso, which include digestive, cleansing, and reproductive organs.

Moonstones calm the emotions and bring about an openness regarding spiritual matters. Gem literature recommends them as stones that heighten psychic abilities, and they are valuable stones in helping people to get in touch with their subconscious nature. Moonstones enable us to find direction and purpose from the subconscious.

In India the Moonstone was believed to bring good fortune and was regarded as sacred. It was never displayed for sale except on a yellow cloth, because yellow is a sacred color. It was given to lovers to arouse passion and to give them the ability to read their own future, good or ill. In order to do this, however, the stone had to be be placed in the mouth while the moon was full.

Antoine Mizauld tells of a Moonstone owned by a traveling friend of his that in-

dicated the waxing and waning of the moon
by a certain white point or mark that grew
or shrank according to the moon's phases.
The owner "vowed and dedicated this
stone to the young king [Edward VI] who
was at that time highly esteemed because
he had good judgement·in regard to rare
and precious things."

Moonstone should be worn as a ring.

It is the birthstone of persons born in
June and has a positive zodiacal affinity for
Libra, Cancer, Scorpio, and Pisces. It is recommended for farmers, artists, dancers,
and young men.

◇ ◇ ◇

Morganite

Morganite is a pink member of the Beryl
family named after, of all people, J. P. Mor-
gan. It is found in the U.S., Brazil, and
U.S.S.R. It is beneficial to the nervous system and can impart a sense of calm to an
otherwise harried existence.

◇ ◇ ◇

Nephrite

(See Jade.)

Obsidian

Obsidian is a black volcanic glass found worldwide. Because of its plentiful nature in ancient civilized areas, it was used often for ornaments, mirrors, knives, and jewelry. It can be flecked with white or striped with an iridescence that gives it a hypnotic, metallic milkiness. Obsidian has been used by American Indian tribes because it is believed to sharpen inner and outer vision.

Obsidian will help keep away negativity and is an extremely protective stone, particularly for sensitive people. Obsidian helps you let go of old loves and old ways. It stimulates the desire to travel and see new horizons. It can also strengthen prophesy.

The Mayans used Obsidian for ceremonial knives, integral to the rituals and sacrifices they performed. Mexicans used it to form images of their god Tezcatlipoca. The name of this divinity is interpreted as "shining mirror," expressed by the brilliant effect of the polished surface of Obsidian. Mirrors of this material are said to have been used for divination in ancient Mexico and neighboring countries.

Obsidian relates well with Scorpios.

Onyx

> A camel's head, or two goats among mortals, if on an onyx, has the power to convoke, assemble and constrain demons: if anyone wears it he will see terrible visions in sleep.
>
> (Ragiel, *Book of Wings*)

Onyx, a secretive stone, varies in color from black or white to translucent with striated layers of red, pink, brown, and yellow. It is found in Italy, United States, and in Mexico, and is commonly used as a building material. Some channelers claim it will be used in the future much as marble is used now. The shapes or patterns that Onyx holds inside it have led some to suggest that Onyx has a picture in it that tells a story or carries a lesson.

Whereas a Moonstone will "remember the spiritual events that happen to a man," an Onyx will retain memory of the physical occurrences surrounding a person. Onyx, often used in jewelry because the supply of this stone is so profuse, is a strong stone to use in psychometry because it tells the story of the wearer. Positively, it is a strength-giving stone, a good stone for athletes or people under extreme mental and emotional stress. Because it brings balance to mind or body as well as strength of mind, it is also a good stone for those who are flighty by nature.

Onyx should always be worn on the left side of the body or, when used by an athlete, worn down the center of the body on a long chain so that it hangs in the area of the solar plexus.

Onyx is a strengthening stone that can help you approach a lesson or task with greater self-confidence. It is in tune with the energies of the earth, and therefore a stone that creates balance and helps you feel more comfortable in your surroundings. It acts as a mental tonic and can benefit those with overwhelming fears and worries. Physically, Onyx is said to be good for the teeth and bones.

Traditionally, Onyx worn on the neck was said to cool the ardors of love. Cardano states that everywhere in India the stone was worn for this purpose. It was commonly believed that Onyx provoked discord and separated lovers—perhaps the layers of black and white in the stone suggested this.

It is highly recommended that Onyx be used in conjunction with Pearl and Diamond.

It has affinities with Aquarius, Pisces, Cancer, and Libra.

◊ ◊ ◊

Opal

Precious Opals are white or milky stones with a pattern of shifting colors inside. Fire

Opals are milky, dense and rarely display opalescence. Common Opals are opaque, without dynamic plays of color, ranging in shades from clear to transparent to yellow-brown. It should be noted that Opals are extremely sensitive and must be treated with great care. They contain up to thirty percent water and if they are cracked, lose the water responsible for their opalescence.

Opals are rarely used in crystal layouts, except by someone who wishes to intensify his or her emotional state. Opals easily diversify and scatter energy, and some gemstone literature states frankly that many who wear this stone have a fickle nature. If you are scattered in thinking and actions, an Opal can certainly magnify this quality, but if you are centered, Opals enable you to look into many subjects. Opals, particularly Fire Opals, are good for business, though they can adversely affect the solar plexus. Anytime the wearer feels uncomfortable with an Opal, the stone should be removed.

Opals can, however, enhance cosmic consciousness and bring joy and creativity. They are sometimes associated with intuition.

Opals are best worn on the little finger, as far away from the body as possible. They should not be worn by teenagers or with other stones. When properly worn, they send out amplified love from the wearer to those nearby.

The *Edda* tells of a sacred stone that the clever smith Volondr (the Scandinavian

Vulcan) formed from the eyes of children. The Brothers Grimm conjectured that this was a round, milk-white Opal. Certainly Opal was often called *ophthalmios*, or eye stone, in the Middle Ages, and it was commonly believed that the image of a boy or girl would be set in the pupil of the eye.

Albertus Magnus describes the Opal thusly:

> The porphanus is a stone which is in the crown of the Roman Emperor, and none like it has ever been seen; for this very reason it is called porphanus. It is of a subtle vinous tinge, and its hue is as though pure white snow flashed and sparkled with the color of bright, ruddy wine and was overcome by this radiance. It is a translucent stone and there is a tradition that formerly it shone in the nighttime, but now, in our age, it does not sparkle in the dark. It is said to guard the regal honor.

Indeed, in the Middle Ages, Opals were said to cure eye diseases, and the magic power of the stone could supposedly render its wearer invisible. Because of this attribute, it was called patron of thieves.

We are told that blond maidens valued nothing more highly than necklaces of Opals, for while they wore these ornaments, their hair was sure to guard its beautiful color.

Although Opal was regarded as a stone of misfortune, black Opal is considered an exceptionally lucky stone. A number of deposits of black Opals were found in the white cliff region of New South Wales, Australia.

It is said that if you dream of Opals, you will receive great possessions.

Pearl

Pearls are calcified objects made by shellfish from the very same material that they use to form their protective shells. Sand or some other foreign material literally gets under the skin of an oyster or other shellfish, and irritates its sensitive skin. In response, the creature coats the offending grain over a period of time with layers of pearly smooth calcium. The result is an object of luminous beauty. Oysters can also be induced to produce Pearls if a grain of sand is purposely forced between the skin and shell. Most Pearls seen today are produced by this method and are known as cultured pearls. Pearls are usually pale white or cream-colored, though darker blue, gray, and even black variations exist.

Pearls are the product of both salt- and freshwater oysters; the freshwater Pearl is more elongated and irregular in shape. Pearls are considered perfect if they have an evenly spherical shape. The less perfectly shaped specimens are equally attractive and much less expensive to purchase.

Pearls have been used for jewelry, closures on clothing, and decorative accents on many surfaces. They vary in size from slightly bigger than a grain of sand to the size of a baseball, though the average Pearl is between a quarter to a half inch in diameter.

Most Pearls available today are cultivated in specially constructed saltwater environments, often in Japan, where the water is warmer and more conducive to their development. In recent years even Japanese pearls have become less available because of increasing ocean pollution. Natural Pearls are virtually nonexistent because of this worldwide abuse of the water by careless industrialized nations.

Pearl necklaces and earrings are the most common form of Pearl jewelry and are considered by many to be the ultimate statement of simple elegance. This, and the economic value of Pearls, have taken much of the focus off healing properties of the Pearl.

Although Pearls take much less time to come into being, as compared to the other gems and minerals, they have the advantage of being formed in sea water, a known purifier. They also become tuned to the phases of the moon, which controls tidal changes.

Oysters are feminine in nature, both in their physical manifestation and in the fact that they contain an embryonic object within them. Pearls are in tune with women, especially pregnant women.

Pearls are absorbing by nature and because of this must be used with caution. If you feel excessively negative while wearing a Pearl, it will hold that energy until it is worn again. Remember, Pearl is the result of layer upon layer of substance produced to combat irritation.

Another quality of the Pearl is its roundness. A perfect sphere is a soft and soothing object. Think of an environment where the problems you encounter are hills of various sizes. Think of a Pearl as rolling over the hills. Take this as an example and learn to overcome problems smoothly. A Pearl is a soothing influence.

Pearl's relation to female qualities also makes it very nurturing. Pearls, if used properly, will lessen stress and its resulting maladies: hypertension, headaches, and exhaustion. This may help to prevent heart attacks and strokes. Pearls are also an aid in digestion and may reduce the chance of developing ulcers.

Traditionally, a Pearl is the symbol of modesty and purity.

If you are using Pearls in conjunction with other gemstones, consider Diamonds to amplify and purify, or Emeralds to bring negative energy out and disperse it.

Pearls can be used by all signs of the zodiac and are often the assigned birthstone of those born in June. Pearls are recommended for occupations as varied as artists, chiropractors, and farmers.

◇ ◇ ◇

Peridot   *use*

Peridot is a very clear, pale green stone that is found in the U.S., Brazil, and Egypt. Peridot's color is a unique frequency, generally yellow (which is stimulating and life-affirming) buffered with blue (spiritual and serene in its effects). This combination produces the delicate green of Peridot.

Peridot's essence lies in its clarity and minimal color. If you are in control of your life and prepared for the future, Peridot is an extremely advantageous stone. It boosts confidence and heightens assertive energy. For those with a lower level of these qualities, Peridot may work too quickly to be comfortable.

Peridot is a visionary stone. It helps connect us to our destinies and to an understanding of the purpose of existence. Peridot is in tune with the higher elements, with the natural progression of events, and the attainment of spiritual truth. It can help us visualize not only the ultimate peak of physical but of spiritual continuation as well. However, if you are confused or fearful, Peridot should be used in a limited way.

Peridot releases toxins and brings them to the surface, thus neutralizing them. It helps with mental cleansing by highlighting problems. The stomach and other digestive tract organs may benefit from

Peridot. It also stimulates tissue regeneration.

Peridot is given to people born in August and is a good stone for Libras and Capricorns.

◇ ◇ ◇

Petrified Wood

Petrified Wood is another example of fossilized plant matter that is used for healing purposes. It has a special relationship to humankind in that trees have circulatory systems that in many ways function like our own. This makes Petrified Wood sympathetic to the maladies of the skin, muscle tissue, and circulatory system.

Petrified Wood usually comes in shades of brown but can also have stripes of black or gray in it. Wood becomes petrified by its mineralization, and these minerals can influence and change the color with time. Petrified Wood is found worldwide.

Athletes are well-advised to carry Petrified Wood with them and use it in healing layouts. Gem literature states that it also benefits people with arterial sclerosis, arthritis, rheumatism, senility, and blood clots.

Because it is an artifact that gives us clues about how life existed in the past, Petrified Wood can help us to investigate past-life experiences. It also has a deep connection to the earth and the environment and will make the user more aware of nature.

◇ ◇ ◇

Platinum

Platinum is a silvery gray metal found in North America, Brazil, and Germany. An expensive and rare metal, it is used by medical science as a replacement for bone, since it is in harmony with the body and will not react chemically with it.

Platinum is generally considered beneficial for people who experience excess in their lives. If any aspect of your life seems extreme or difficult to control, Platinum will slow things down and allow you to take greater control.

Platinum's benefits extend to several systems of the body. It helps to keep hormonal and chemical levels balanced, aids in the transmission of nerve impulses, and may make the heart and circulatory system more efficient.

According to gem literature, Platinum is also particularly suited to aiding the functions of the brain, improving the memory. It will also improve your attitude and outlook on life in general.

Platinum is often used in jewelry but is best worn on the little finger.

Pyrite

Pyrite is a mineralized crystal that forms in clusters of metalliclike cubes. Its color varies from a bright gold or brass to shades of copper or green. It is found in most of North America as well as in Chile and Peru. Because of its bright, shiny nature, it is often mistaken by amateur prospectors for gold, hence its nickname, "fool's gold."

Pyrite is beneficial to the respiratory and circulatory systems. Because it contains iron, it is very connected to the transfer of oxygen from the lungs to the bloodstream. Pyrite helps the skin protect itself from the elements, and also aids the digestive tract, lessening irritation by ingested toxins.

The most important gift of Pyrite, though, is its ability to aid mental capacity. The physical structure of Pyrite is geometrically precise, even though the individual cubes are of varying size and distribution. By combining this natural randomness with geometric precision, Pyrite maintains a unique stability. Pyrite helps to balance creative and intuitive impulses with scientific and practical ones. Communication skills can also improve with the help of Pyrite, which eases anxiety and frustration.

Crystals of Iron Pyrite (native iron disulphide) are sometimes used as amulets by the North American Indians.

In ancient Mexico, Pyrite was valued for its reflective qualities. The Mexicans made mirrors of Pyrite by polishing one flat side and carving the other into a convex shape. Frequently the convex side was embellished with a symbolic representation.

Pyrite is strongly suggested for people who tackle large conceptual ideas in business, the arts, or education. It is effective in attracting money to its owner.

The stimulation of the mind can be enhanced by using Pyrite in conjunction with Fluorite and Calcite.

Quartz

Many of the New Age and homeopathic/holistic approaches to healing are centered around the Quartz crystal. Quartz encompasses a large family of stones and crystals, all of which are made up primarily of silicon dioxide, one of the most common and most important substances in the world. Crystals of pure Quartz, generally six-sided, can be found in all shades and colors. Quartz crystals grow singularly or in groups and take on different shapes according to the temperature at the time of their formation. Quartz crystals can also contain other minerals "frozen" within, as in Rutilated Quartz. Quartz can be formed of microscopic crystals and take on entirely different appearances and qualities.

Other members of the Quartz family include Chalcedony, Agate, Jasper, Carnelian, Onyx, and Sardonyx. These are treated separately because their healing qualities are very different from crystal Quartz.

Crystal Quartz has scientific as well as healing value. Quartz, when cut properly, can generate electromagnetic energy in response to applied pressure. Conversely, it will vibrate at radio frequencies when electricity is applied to it. This marvelous ability to store, release, and regulate energy has made Quartz the basis for the electronic revolution. Silica, or silicon dioxide, the chemical name for Quartz, is the main component of all computer chips.

Consider, then, the potential Quartz crystal has as a healer. All the functions it performs for modern civilization only hint at its full potential. In all its forms Quartz helps heal the mental, physical, and spiritual ailments that have plagued humankind for centuries.

Clear Quartz (Rock Crystal or White Quartz)

Clear Quartz crystal, sometimes called Rock Crystal, is a dedicated healer. Pure white light passes through it easily, leaving all the colors of the spectrum unaltered and giving substance to the argument that Clear Quartz crystals can help balance all the elements needed to make us whole and fulfilled. Clear crystals also amplify whatever influences are present in an individual or location. Any deficiency present will become visible and obvious.

Clear Quartz acts as a purifier and tunes into the frequency of each individual. It works at a vibrational level to return the body to its least altered or diseased state. If specific areas or organs are blocked from transmitting or receiving the flow of energy throughout the body, Clear Quartz will unblock them. Thus Clear Quartz crystals play an important role in creating harmony and helping to balance all stimuli, positive and negative.

In spiritual matters, Quartz crystal is helpful in guiding our search for the meaning and importance of existence. Clear Quartz crystal can help us tune into our own energy and filter out unnecessary distraction, thus aiding meditation.

The origin of Clear Quartz was somewhat of a mystery to the ancients. St. Jerome, quoting Pliny, explains its formation as a congelation of water in dark caverns of the mountains where the temperature is so cold that "while a stone to the touch, it seems like water to the eye." Quartz came to symbolize freedom and purity of faith to those in the Church.

In Japan, Clear Quartz is considered to be the congealed breath of the White Dragon. Larger, more brilliant specimens are said to be the saliva of the Violet Dragon. In Japanese mythology the dragon is emblematic of the powers of creation, and this indicates the esteem in which Clear Quartz was held by the Japanese.

The term *suisho*, used both in China and Japan to designate Clear Quartz, reflects the ancient idea that Quartz was ice so long congealed that it could not be liquified.

For the Japanese, Clear Quartz is the perfect jewel, a symbol of purity, the infinity of space, and also of patience and perseverance.

Clear Quartz can be carried or worn by anyone and used in conjunction with any other stone or gem for specific physical problems: it will amplify the effects of individual stones and attune the treatment to the energy of an individual person.

Window Crystals and Other Esoteric Variations

Window crystals are an unusual variation of Quartz. Even though each crystal has the basic six-sided crystal shape and may be terminated, there is an additional flat plane, usually diamond-shaped, that gives a view of the inner chamber of the crystal.

What this crystal teaches us is the importance of looking within ourselves, even if the view into our own soul is clouded and imperfect. In fact, if someone chooses a crystal with elements that obscure its clarity, it may be a sign that there are elements within the person that need clarifying.

Dendritic Quartz is another variation that, much like Moss Agate, has pictures on its surface. These shapes often resemble plants or animals.

Elestial crystals are crystals that generally have fewer side planes and blunt ends. These crystals are young and usually much smaller than most other Quartz crystals.

Phantom crystals are crystals that at one point finished their growth cycle, then began growing again later. When looking inside these crystals, you can see a striation that indicates where the original tip was. For someone drawn to this type of stone, a need for growth is indicated.

Singing crystals have small side projections off the main crystal. These crystals produce a pleasant tone when struck by another crystal, hence the name "singing."

Single- and Double-Terminated Clear Quartz

Single-terminated Clear Quartz crystals are six-sided with a flat bottom and point at the top. These crystals teach us to focus energy on a concentrated point. These are especially useful for people who have a specific area or organ in the body that needs lots of attention. For mental states, it will help you to focus on the best path to travel in breaking old habits or establishing new ones.

Double-terminated Clear Quartz crystals are a special occurrence in nature. Most terminated crystals grow out of rock, often in clusters with other crystals. Double-terminated Clear Quartz crystals grow in clay or other soft materials. A Double-terminated crystal has a point on both ends, which gives it expanded qualities.

Double-terminated crystals can draw energy as well as direct it. The center of the crystal works like a neutralizing chamber. One of the points draws negative energy inside, where it is transformed and purified. The energy then passes out of the crystal through both points. The Double-terminated crystal shows us that the most efficient energy comes from our own center.

Amethyst

Amethyst is a violet-colored Quartz stone found in Brazil, Canada, Sri Lanka, and parts of East Africa. Its color varies from a deep violet to pale lavender, almost to the point of being clear. For centuries Amethyst has been valued as a jewel and, before the discovery of large deposits of the stone in Brazil, was considered a precious gem. Its curative properties have long been recognized by natural healers and psychics. Amethyst has a direct link to the mind; Edgar Cayce suggested it for control of temperament.

Amethyst bolsters the production of the hormones, and strengthens the cleansing organs, the circulatory system and blood, the immune system, and body metabolism.

Few crystals offer as much potential benefit to the mind as Amethyst. It soothes the nervous system and aids in the transmission of neural signals. Amethyst helps you feel less scattered and more in control of your faculties. This allows you to center and balance excessive emotional highs and lows. Amethyst helps the user feel more able to rely on his or her intuition. Memory skills and motivation improve. Goals are clearer, more realistic, and easier to achieve. However, you must use this stone cautiously with subjects who have paranoid or schizoid tendencies.

Amethyst can benefit people with insomnia or troubled sleep. Because of its ability to soothe the mind and focus attention, Amethyst is ideal for those who meditate.

Amethyst encourages the love of God and promotes selflessness. It is useful in dispelling rage, anger, fear, and anxiety, and is a good stone for clarifying and remembering dreams. Amethyst also helps relieve physical and emotional pain.

Old gem tracts suggest:

From passion and from care kept free
Shall Pisces children ever be
Who wear so all the world may see.
                              (The Amethyst)

Traditionally, Amethyst was recommended as a cure for drunkenness. An Amethyst worn on the person was said to have a sobering effect not only upon those who had partaken too freely of the cup that intoxicates but also upon those overcome by physical passion.

In the fifteenth century Amethyst was believed to have the power to control evil thoughts, quicken the intelligence, and render men shrewd in business matters. It was also believed to preserve soldiers from harm and give them victory over their enemies. It was recommended to hunters to facilitate capture of wild animals, and, of course, it shared with many other stones the power to preserve the wearer from contagion.

French literature states that the god Bacchus, offended at some slight, was determined to avenge himself and declared that the first person he should meet when he and his train passed by should be devoured by his tigers. But fate willed it that this luckless mortal was a beautiful and pure maiden named Amethyst, on her way to worship at the shrine of Diana. As the ferocious beasts sprang toward her, she sought the protection of the goddess and was saved by changing shape into a pure white stone. Recognizing the miracle and repenting his cruelty, Bacchus poured the juice of the grape as a libation over the petrified body of the maiden, thus giving to the stone the violet hue.

For best effect, Amethyst should be moved around the body, particularly in the lung area. If it is to be worn, it should be worn over the heart or at the throat. From time to time, as it feels comfortable to the wearer, the stone should be removed.

When using Amethyst in conjunction with other stones or crystals, Rose Quartz is strongly recommended. Amethysts are recommended for dancers and optometrists.

It responds well to Pisces, Aries, Sagittarius, and Capricorn.

Aventurine

Aventurine is a crystal with very positive qualities. In ancient Tibet it was used for nearsightedness, improving the wearer's perception, and stimulating creativity. It is found in shades of blue, brown, red, and green. The green is generally recognized as the crystal with the most varied uses. It can be found in the U.S.S.R., Brazil, India, and Nepal.

Aventurine is supposed beneficial to the thymus gland, the nervous system, and one's general state of mind. It can be placed anywhere on the body for healing purposes or simply carried around wherever you go. It influences both physical and mental planes, with the ability to diffuse a negative situation and bring it into balance. Aventurine promotes a state of general well-being.

If used in conjunction with Malachite, Aventurine can help clear mental or emotional blocks by raising them to the surface of consciousness. If used with Rose Quartz, it will increase your ability for empathy and love. In general, either of these combinations will align the emotions with the body and intellect and bring about a more balanced day-to-day existence.

Considering Aventurine's natural affinity with the thymus gland, it is not surprising that this crystal helps promote proper

growth during the first seven y
child's development (this is when
mus is most active). Its ability to
and balance has a very positive in
during this period of constant discovery
and stimulation.

Aventurine is a gentle, important healer.
From childhood to maturity it can impart
a positive influence in every aspect of your
life.

Blue Quartz

Blue Quartz, a fairly rare stone, is found in
the United States and Brazil. It varies in
color from pale blue to lavender or gray. It
has beneficial effects for the upper torso
and related organs.

Blue Quartz helps purify the bloodstream
and heighten the body's immunity to disease. As with other blue stones or gems,
it can help you discover or increase your
understanding of your spiritual nature.
Blue Quartz has a calming effect upon the
mind and stimulates hope.

Citrine Quartz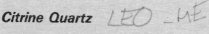

Citrine Quartz is an energizing and highly
beneficial crystal. Its color is usually a pale
golden yellow, but it can be found in darker
shades as well, although some gem literature considers the darkest crystals to be
Smoky Quartz. The Celtic people of Scotland call the dark Citrine crystals Morion
and Cairngorm.

...itrine's energies are directly related to the sun and, like the sun, are invigorating and positive. Citrine can surround and fill anyone with its brilliant color, energizing every aspect of life. Its energy increases motivation and promotes physical activity, which in turn improves digestion and helps the cleansing organs. Citrine may also work as a detoxifier for the blood.

Persons involved with education or business will especially benefit from the positive energy that emanates from Citrine.

Citrine can guide you to harness and utilize your creative energy. Citrine helps us analyze events and steer them in a positive direction. It develops inner calm and security, and makes us less sensitive and more open to constructive criticism. Citrine can dispel negative feelings and help us to accept the flow of events.

Citrine Quartz has a zodiacal affinity with Leo and Virgo.

Herkimer Diamond

Herkimer Diamonds derive their name from the fact that they are found only in Herkimer, New York. These clear crystals closely resemble Diamonds but are really Quartz. However, they are similar to Diamonds in that they help to increase the energy and healing qualities of other stones.

Herkimer Diamonds are especially clear and refract light internally, allowing you to see rainbows within the crystal. Herkimer Diamonds are very useful in helping to lessen the pressures of day-to-day life and the stress- and tension-related diseases that can result. The stones do this by helping you recognize the signs of stress before it can do physical damage. Herkimer Diamonds can help you choose a direction to follow that will offer the path of least resistance, thus preventing negative energy and tension from gaining a foothold.

Herkimer Diamonds work as auxiliary filters that accent the natural filtering abilities of the body. If a person is in good physical and mental health, the body naturally filters out toxins before they can be damaging. However, if a person is unhealthy, his or her defenses need a boost. Herkimer Diamonds can add that boost.

Herkimer Diamonds are very old stones. They contain a store of ecological memory that can be utilized by a person who can tune into the energy. They can also guide you in remembering your own past-life experiences.

Herkimer Diamonds can be worn or carried anywhere and are strongly suggested for pendants or earrings.

Purple Quartz

This stone should not be confused with Amethyst. It has a dark violet color and may have inclusions or clouding within it. It is beneficial to the cleansing organs. Purple Quartz is capable of stimulating thoughts and helping you learn to contemplate and analyze data. This meditative quality helps you learn to feel less threatened by events over which you have no control.

Rose Quartz

Rose Quartz is deeply in tune with emotional states. This pleasant-looking pink stone is found in the United States, Brazil, and Japan. Its value as a nurturing friend cannot be overstated. Gentleness and love play a large part in the healing capabilities of Rose Quartz. A soothing influence, it softens the edges of our existence and makes negative influences or experiences less detrimental.

Rose Quartz deals with energy on an emotional level. Although it may seem odd to give an inanimate object emotional characteristics, Rose Quartz does have a sympathetic nature and when it is in tune with its owner's emotions, it helps diffuse negative stimuli and uncomfortable memories.

Rose Quartz helps us discover the ability to love ourselves and makes us more open to other people. It is of particular value in helping us to forgive ourselves, hastening self-acceptance. It helps us realize that all change is important, even difficult change. Rose Quartz stimulates love and tender appreciation of all things. If you are troubled by something, it can help you find a space within yourself to accept the situation, find respite, and restore your faith.

Rose Quartz is advantageous for the heart and circulatory systems. It also helps the cleansing organs. The reproductive organs may become healthier and more in tune with the positive energy we need for fulfilling expressions of love and tenderness. As we become more positive and responsive to the needs of others, the physical expression of love increases as well. Rose Quartz is said to help increase fertility.

Rose Quartz is an excellent gift for expressing love and will positively affect whomever it is given to. It is suggested for children because it helps to develop a nurturing and compassionate spirit.

Rose Quartz is recommended for artists, acupuncturists, lecturers, and those suffering from low self-esteem.

If worn, Rose Quartz works well as a necklace. It should rest over the heart.

Rose Quartz will benefit all signs of the zodiac.

Rutilated Quartz

Rutilated Quartz contains Rutile in needle-like mineral inclusions. The rutilation manifests itself in interesting random patterns that, besides being pleasant to look at, help focus the healing qualities of the crystal. One can find Rutilated versions of most of the types of Quartz discussed thus far.

The primary reason to consider applying a Rutilated Quartz is that it heightens whatever energetic influence the regular

Quartz possesses and helps direct that boosted energy to problematic areas.

Smoky Quartz - CHECK

Smoky Quartz is a medium-to-dark brown crystal found in the United States, Brazil, and Scotland. A word of warning is in order regarding choosing Smoky Quartz crystals. Its dark color is caused by impurities, usually carbon, iron, or titanium. But the color of some Smoky Quartz is caused by the effects of minute amounts of decaying radium, within the crystal itself. Because of the presence of this natural low-grade radiation, Smoky Quartz is good for people with radiation-related illness or those in chemotherapy. However, some of these stones, although posing no health danger, are heavily radiated and therefore have different healing qualities from most Smoky Quartz. It is best to avoid these heavily irradiated crystals. Most gemstone and crystal stores do not sell them, and most gem experts advise against using them in layouts.

Natural Smoky Quartz crystals, like other brown stones, are closely in tune with the anchoring energy of the earth. They are often used for ailments of the lower torso. The reproductive organs, muscle tissue, heart, and nervous system all profit from Smoky Quartz's presence. Smoky Quartz's connection to the earth also heightens your understanding of nature and concern for the environment.

Smoky Quartz is different from many other stones in its ability to neutralize negative influences. It is a passive means to change, useful when caution is necessary or gradual change is called for.

Smoky Quartz was often used in crystal gazing.

It has affinities with all signs of the zodiac.

Tiger's Eye Quartz

Tiger's Eye, sometimes called Cat's Eye, is a common form of Quartz that has been popular in jewelry making for years. It comes in various shades of light or dark brown and has fibrous inclusions that add a luminosity to the stone. Tiger's Eye does resemble a feline eye if properly cut and polished.

Tiger's Eye has the grounding energy of the earth, but this is embellished with a glowing warmth, the influence of the yellow/gold highlights of the fibrous inclusions.

This is a stone for people who need more confidence to accomplish their goals. Tiger's Eye helps us recognize the resources within ourselves and use those resources for the attainment of our dreams. It helps us judge a situation and determine how best to approach it.

Because of the many inclusions in Tiger's Eye and its almost iridescent appearance, light refraction plays an important role in how one views the stone. Its appearance is constantly varying, just as most people vary in their appearance to others. Tiger's Eye can help a user find the most advantageous and positive way to reveal his or her inner energy and light.

Tiger's Eye draws helpful people and material things to the wearer. Some gemstone literature also states that Tiger's Eye centers energy and mental focus.

Cat's Eye was used by the natives of Ceylon as a charm against evil spirits.

The stone should be set in copper or silver and worn on the right arm.

Tourmalinated Quartz

This is another type of included Quartz. The most common inclusion is Black Tourmaline. This combination produces a balance between contrasting elements. Tourmalinated Quartz illustrates for us the inevitability of new and seemingly opposite elements working together. We all have within ourselves elements that seem to conflict but that can be made to work together harmoniously. Tourmalinated Quartz will help this process.

$\diamond \ \diamond \ \diamond$

Rhodochrosite

Rhodochrosite is a fairly recent discovery in the mineral kingdom. It comes in shades of orange and pink, and has stripes of various width in shades of white. Most Rhodochrosite comes from the United States or U.S.S.R.

Rhodochrosite is a very beneficial stone for those with asthma or other respiratory illnesses. It has a soothing and warming energy that helps you filter out the irritants that trigger respiratory difficulty. This also applies to the purification of the circulatory system and the cleansing organs, especially the kidneys.

Rhodochrosite can help you alleviate irrational fears and paranoia. This ability to "see" things less negatively can also affect the eyes in a physical sense. Rhodochrosite will enhance the dream state, resulting in better sleep.

Gem literature suggests using Rhodochrosite in conjunction with Malachite or Copper. If worn, Rhodochrosite is most beneficial as a bracelet.

It is suggested for those born under the sign of Cancer.

Rhodonite

Rhodonite is a stone found in the United States, Brazil, India, Japan, and U.S.S.R. It varies in color from pink to red to brown.

Gem literature states its use for trauma, confusion, and confidence. Rhodonite has a very beneficial effect upon the growth of bones and the hearing system. It fine-tunes audio capabilities, which makes it an advantageous stone for musicians and sound technicians.

If worn, Rhodonite works well as a necklace.

Rock Crystal

(See Clear Quartz.)

Rubelite

(See Pink Tourmaline.)

Ruby

Ruby is a gemstone that must be carefully scrutinized before choosing it for healing purposes. The classic stone is usually a deep, brilliant red but can be found in shades of pink or lavender. Rubies are found in the United States, India, and Sri Lanka. It is a powerful stone whose stimulating energy can bring startling things to light. Like the Diamond, it is an amplifier of energy—both positive and negative.

Red is commonly interpreted as a passionate color, and sometimes Ruby's effect is like waving a red cape to invite a bull. Ruby can bring anger or negativity to the surface quickly. For this reason it should be used with a knowledge of how to gain from the experience. Otherwise you are likely to be overcome by the passion it stirs up. Remember that Ruby brings negativity to the surface to be burned away or dispelled. Allow yourself to be purified by the experience, not overwhelmed.

A Ruby can also amplify positive energy, heightening whatever purity you already possess. This positive energy can sometimes form a supply of energy one can draw upon when dealing with the negative issues Ruby can stir up.

Rubies help us in all matters of love, including love of ourselves. They benefit the heart and circulatory system, and can assist in the filtration and detoxification of the body. Gem literature also suggests Rubies for the eyes.

The Ruby is an energizing stone that stimulates motivation and visualization. They can help the user be more realistic about goals and more honest with intentions.

Rubies were valued above all other stones by Hindus because they preserved the bodily and mental health of the wearer by removing evil thoughts, controlling amorous desires, dissipating pestilential vapors, and reconciling disputes.

In the *Lapidary* of Philippe de Valois, it is said, "The books tell us the beautiful clear and fine Ruby is the lord of stones; it is the gem of gems, and surpasses all other precious stones in virtue."

A fourteenth-century treatise attributed

to Sir John Mandeville assures a fortunate owner of a brilliant Ruby that he will live in peace and concord with all men, that neither his land nor his rank will be taken from him, and that he will be preserved from all perils. The magic of the stone would also guard his house, fruit trees, and vineyards from injury by tempests. All these good effects were best secured if the Ruby, set in ring, bracelet, or brooch, were worn on the left side.

In Burma, Rubies were valued for invulnerability. In order to attain this end, however, a Ruby had to be inserted into the flesh so that it could become part of the body. Those who imbedded Rubies in their skin believed they could become invincible to any wounds caused by spears, swords, or guns. It is well known that some reckless soldiers pass relatively unharmed through many dangers of war and therefore it is easy to understand how this superstition may have sometimes appeared to have been verified.

Rubies should be worn as a brooch, ring, or anklet. They should be kept away from the solar plexus.

The Ruby is the assigned birthstone of those born in July and has affinity with those born under the signs of Sagittarius, Leo, Capricorn, and Scorpio.

◊ ◊ ◊

Rutile

Rutile is usually found as a large, black, prismatic crystal, although it has many forms and can come in shades of blue, gray, red, and brown. A common stone composed mainly of titanium oxide, it is prevalent in igneous and metamorphic rock formations worldwide. Rutile also occurs as needle-thin crystal inclusions in Rutilated Quartz.

Rutile filters out memories of the past that have a negative effect upon the present. It is a mediator in self-confrontation and can neutralize feelings of self-contempt.

◊ ◊ ◊

Sapphire

Sapphire is a serene stone. When most people discuss Sapphires, they are referring to the beautiful deep blue Sapphire, but the stone also comes in shades of gray, black, yellow, and green. Sapphires are found in the United States, Australia, and India.

The best way to describe the stone is by comparing it to the beauty of the night sky. Sapphire has the serenity, endless quiet, and calm of a peaceful view from a remote mountaintop. You can bask in its soothing environment and let distraction and negative energy flow away. Sapphires help you find the best way to contemplate the peacefulness of existence. Sapphires lessen tension and align the mental, physical, and spiritual planes.

Sapphire can be an important stone for people with spiritual confusion or depression, those involved in situations out of their control, and anyone with concentration problems. Sapphire will help you get more in touch with your true essence and help you understand your role in the workings of the universe. People who meditate will find Sapphire a helpful stone.

Illness or disease are often the result of an imbalance within the body. Sapphire can help to restore this balance through its ability to ease stress and tension.

The usefulness of Sapphire as an eye stone for the removal of all impurities or foreign bodies was noted by Albertus Magnus, who writes that he had seen it employed for this purpose. He added that when a Sapphire is used in this way, it should be dipped in cold water both before and after the operation. (This precaution was probably intended as a way to cleanse the stone, a necessity when a variety of people suffering from contagious diseases of the eyes used the same stone.)

The proper method of applying a Sapphire to cure plague boils is detailed at some length by Von Helmont. A gem of fine, deep color was to be selected and rubbed gently and slowly around the pestilential tumor. During and immediately after this operation the patient would feel little alleviation, but a good while after the removal of the stone, favorable symptoms would appear, provided the malady were not too far advanced. This ability was attributed to a magnetic force in Sapphire by means of which the absent gem then continued to extract "the pestilential virulence and contagious poison from the infected part."

Damigeron notes that Sapphire is a regal gem and asserts that kings wore it about their neck as a powerful defense against harm. It was said to preserve its wearer from envy and also to attract divine favor. Legend and tradition claim that the law given to Moses was engraved on tablets of Sapphire (however, the tablets were probably of Lapis Lazuli because Sapphire does not come in the size necessary to engrave such a list).

The Bishop of Rennes, in the twelfth century, lavished praise upon Sapphire and recommended its use in rings (at that time the stone was favored in ecclesiastical rings because of its affinity to the sky). It was also said to banish fraud and was valued by necromancers for its ability to help them hear and understand particularly obscure oracles. Like the Emerald, it was considered an antidote against poison.

Black Sapphires are the most protective of all Sapphire colors. All Sapphires are best worn as rings.

Sapphire is suggested for Gemini, Virgo, Libra, Taurus, and Capricorn. It is recommended for healers and those involved in mental pursuits.

◇ ◇ ◇

Sard

Sard is a porous brick-red member of the Chalcedony family that is found in the United States and India. It is not generally considered to be a strong healer, though it does possess limited properties similar to Carnelians. Some healers suggest it for open wounds and conditions of the blood. It can be beneficial to the cleansing organs and in strengthening to the mind.

Traditionally Sard was regarded as protection against incantations and sorcery, and was believed to sharpen the wits of the wearer, rendering him fearless, victorious, and happy. The red hue of this stone was considered able to neutralize the malign influence of the dark Onyx, driving away bad dreams and dispelling the melancholy thoughts Onyx was capable of inspiring.

◇ ◇ ◇

Sardonyx

Sardonyx is a layered combination of Sard and Onyx, both of which belong to the Chalcedony family. It can include shades of red, brown, black, or white. It is found in Brazil and India.

This stone is best known for its effect upon the bones and lungs. Gem literature recommends its use for depression and in matters of love. Edgar Cayce recommended Sardonyx for its ability to help one achieve greater self-control.

When using Sardonyx, take care to consider the color combination of the stone. Red stimulates, brown is grounding, black is absorbing, and white is purifying. The colors do not cancel each other out. They do, however, buffer each other and maintain a median balance that allows you to affect change.

Sardonyx is recommended for explorers, those engaged in combat, and executives. Sardonyx is a birthstone of those born in August.

Serpentine

Serpentine is a green or yellow stone found in North America, England, and Italy. It is a general detoxifier for the body and helps all the organs of the cleansing system. Serpentine is also beneficial to the blood.

Serpentine can help you feel more in control of life. Gem literature suggests Serpentine for those who wish to heighten psychic abilities and gain greater understanding of the spiritual aspect of existence.

Black Serpentine was used for seals in the fourth and fifth century B.C.

Italian peasants believed that pebbles of green Serpentine could afford protection from the bites of venomous animals (probably because the stripes on the surface of the stone resemble snakeskin). As in the case of Coral, the Italians also believed it should be used in its natural state, probably due to the superstition that iron instruments destroyed magic.

The Irish often carved Serpentine, termed by them Connamara, into pins and broaches.

◇ ◇ ◇

Silver

Silver is a good metal for healing purposes because it is in tune with the energies of the body. The dental and medical professions have both used Silver with great success for a wide variety of reconstructive implants.

Silver works best as a communicator. It should be worn only when it feels right. Silver benefits the circulation and detoxifies the blood. It helps the body recognize imbalances or high levels of hormones and chemicals more readily, enabling them to be naturally corrected. Silver helps the lungs and throat and reduces irritation by pollutants and other impurities in the air. The physical functions of the brain will work with greater ease because silver improves the transmission of nerve impulses.

People with degenerative brain disease, poor memory, irrational fears, and emotional imbalance should strongly consider silver. It aids in verbal and representational communication. Like Gold, Silver helps balance the functions of both sides of the brain.

Silver can be worn as a belt buckle to improve fertility. It can help resolve sexual problems that result from dysfunction or impotence.

Mental activity is clarified and you may notice an increase in your ability to approach intellectual problems. Silver is also known to lessen anxiety over problem-solving.

Gem literature suggests using Silver in conjunction with Agate, Jet, Moonstone, and Turquoise.

Smithsonite

Smithsonite is named for James Smithson, the founder of the Smithsonian Institution. It comes in shades of blue, yellow, pink, green, and purple, and is found in the United States, Australia, Greece, and Italy. Little is known about its healing properties, but gem literature suggests it for security and a balanced life. It will also help you deal with difficult relationships.

Sodalite

Sodalite is a blue stone found in North America as well as in Brazil and France. It can strongly affect changes in your attitude about yourself. Like many other blue stones, it helps you be more objective and less critical about ways of dealing with existence. It helps untangle its user from the entrapments of a complicated life-style. It further teaches an examination of goals once they have been reached.

Gem literature suggests Sodalite for balancing the metabolism. It is beneficial for the cleansing organs and can boost the immune system.

Sodalite is said to be effective in combating the effects of natural and artificial radiation and is recommended for those who work around X-ray equipment or are involved with radioactive material.

It has affinity with those born under the sign of Sagittarius. It is also recommended for those involved in acupuncture.

Spinel

Spinel is a red, green, or blue stone found in the United States, U.S.S.R., Sri Lanka, Italy, and Germany. It encourages moderation of all excesses and aids in the detoxification of both the blood and the mind. If you are too anxious or fear the future, Spinel can help you lessen those anxieties. The skin will also benefit from the use of Spinel.

Spinel is said to be an aid in fasting.

Spinel was probably the famous "marvelous stone" taken from the Lydian river Timolus. Said to change color four times a day, the Lydian stone could be found only by innocent young girls. While they wore it they were protected from outrage.

Star Sapphire

Star Sapphire, similar in ability to the Blue Sapphire, differs in that it has an aqueous inclusion in its makeup that creates a refracted five-pointed star on the stone's surface. This star is a focus point in the gem. It doesn't concentrate the Star Sapphire's energies but rather gives you a focal point that then draws you into the stone's serenity. The star is an example of the principle that all energy radiates out from a center and if we can find that center point within ourselves, we can ourselves radiate calm, positive energy. Star Sapphire is recommended for people who wish to awaken or heighten their psychic abilities.

Star Sapphire works as a relaxing agent during times of extreme physical exertion.

Healers of the spirit and body are often drawn to this stone.

Generally, the color of Star Sapphires is impure. They rarely possess the deep blue color of the fine Blue Sapphire and tend toward milky or gray-blue. The Cingalese used Star Sapphires to protect and guard against witchcraft as Agates were used in other countries to protect against the evil eye.

Sir Richard Burton, known for being a great Oriental traveler, referred to the Star Sapphire he always carried with him as his talisman, claiming it always brought him good horses and prompt attention. Lest anyone jump to conclusions, he stated that it was only in places where he was given proper attention that he showed his gem-stone to the natives, a favor greatly appreciated due to the belief that the sight of a Star Sapphire brought good luck.

Star Sapphire was sometimes called the "stone of destiny," since the three cross-bars on its surface were believed to represent Faith, Hope, and Destiny. It is unique among talismanic stones in that it continues to influence its previous owner even after it is passed onto others.

Star Sapphires, like all Sapphires, should be worn as a ring. It should not be worn as a necklace over the chest area because it can draw the problems of other people toward the user.

◇ ◇ ◇

Topaz — ME — LEO

Topaz is an empathetic stone that gives out its warm glow quite readily. The most common Topaz has a radiant yellow color, but it can also be found in shades of green, blue, and brown. Topaz is mined in the United States, Mexico, Brazil, and Sri Lanka.

When using Topaz, think of it in terms of the sun, sending out rays of warmth and light that are soothing, healing, and life-giving. The color yellow is stimulating but in a way that is very mellow. Topaz sends out its golden rays of energy in all directions. Its benevolent nature sends out its gift of positive energy to all who need it. Topaz is for those in crisis or in need of motivation. It recharges and increases the user's energy level.

Topaz radiates in all directions equally, and you should learn from its example to project your own vision in more than one direction. People who are problem solvers, such as those involved with the arts or science, will benefit from Topaz.

Topaz is an excellent stone for relaxation and comfort. It calms the nervous system and lessens tension, helping the user to become complete and satisfied. The blood will also benefit from the use of Topaz.

Topaz also sheds light on the path to your goals. It pierces the clouds that obscure inner vision and helps light up the correct direction to pursue.

Topaz helps tap our natural resources and allows us to experience the joy of infinity. It makes us appreciate sharing the gift of life. Those in tune with Topaz's positive energy will feel limitless and philanthropic. They will experience an increase in their personal abilities.

St. Hildegard recommended the use of Topaz to cure dimness of vision. The stone was to be placed in wine and left for three days and three nights. Then, upon retiring, the patient was told to rub his or her eyes with the moistened Topaz in such a way that the moisture lightly touched the eyeball. The wine could be used for five days after the stone had been removed. Presumably it was to be drunk by the patient. This story is one of the first references to the use of gem elixirs.

A fifteenth-century Roman physician was reputed to have wrought many wonderful cures of those stricken by plague by touching plague sores with a Topaz that had been owned by two Popes, Clement VI and Gregory II. The fact that this stone had been owned by two pontiffs must have added much to the faith of those exposed to its "curative" powers.

Topaz is best worn as a ring and is beneficial for those born under the signs of Leo, Aries, Sagittarius, and Gemini.

Tourmaline

Tourmaline is a cleanser that works hard to purify one's entire existence. Tourmaline encompasses a large family of stones including Black, Blue, Cat's Eye, Green, Opalized, Red, and Watermelon. Tourmalines are found in the United States, Australia, Brazil, Mexico, and U.S.S.R.

Tourmaline rids the user of specific problem-causing elements. It diffuses and dissipates the effects of negative energy on individual existence and brings about clarity and calmness. It will help the body to function without strain.

Tourmaline generally focuses its effects on specific problem areas, but it is also capable of working in a general way as a cleanser.

In a spiritual sense Tourmaline helps us gain a more balanced understanding of the purpose for existence. Tourmaline won't give answers, but it is capable of bringing to light startling, occasionally painful, information.

Tourmalines have a curious and unique property that may explain their focusing power. When heated, a Tourmaline crystal will develop opposing electrical charges at opposite ends of the crystal.

Tourmaline is a birthstone for people born in October.

Black Tourmaline

Black Tourmaline is much different from other black stones in that it does not absorb negative energy. In fact, it repels it. As a result, many gem experts suggest carrying this stone when you feel surrounded by negativity. It is a valuable stone for crises and for periods of extreme stress.

Black Tourmaline also helps you defend against debilitating diseases. Diseases that have life-threatening crisis points or that do sustained damage over long periods of times, such as heart disease or arthritis, would be well combated with Black Tourmaline. It is also strongly suggested for persons with weakened immune systems.

Black Tourmaline is sometimes found embedded in Clear Quartz (see Tourmalinated Quartz).

Blue Tourmaline (Indocolite)

Blue Tourmaline has the same basic qualities as Green, Red, or Watermelon Tourmaline although it does especially benefit the upper torso, the pulmonary system, and the immune system. If you feel more drawn to Blue Tourmaline over the other Tourmalines, it would be best to follow that intuition. Some believe this stone has a religious nature and that its purpose is to teach spiritual oneness.

Cat's Eye Tourmaline

Little information exists concerning Cat's Eye Tourmaline. Gem literature suggests that it is a lesser healer because of its inclusions. It further states that derived benefits take place over a long period of time. Use this stone only if you are very drawn to it.

Clear Tourmaline

This stone has many of the qualities of the other Tourmalines but in a more low-key manner. Its lack of color is indicative of purity. Clear Tourmaline is beneficial for the immune system and for detoxification of the entire body. Gem literature suggests it for the eyes and for nervous disorders such as epilepsy.

Green Tourmaline

Green Tourmaline is a healing stone that some gem healers consider the strongest of all green stones. It helps achieve balance in all areas.

Green Tourmaline is extremely beneficial for the nervous system, the brain, and the immunological system. It gives you a highly refined sense of how to best recognize and deal with a problem. It is also a stone that stimulates creativity and communication. Energetic and rejuvenating, it helps you follow through with a problem to its conclusion. Green Tourmaline also helps you recognize and avoid negative energies before they become damaging. This can benefit anyone who is involved with a career.

Gem literature recommends Green Tourmaline for people who wish to better understand their own spirituality.

Green Tourmaline has an affinity for Scorpio, Capricorn, Cancer, and Pisces.

Opalized Tourmaline

Opalized Tourmaline is almost the reverse of Cat's Eye Tourmaline. The inclusion, resulting from water, heightens the effects of the stone. The additional refraction of light helps intensify the healing energy, accelerating its benefits. This stone, though rare, is a valuable addition to one's collection of healing stones.

Pink Tourmaline (Rubelite)

Pink Tourmaline comes in shades ranging from pale pink to salmon, and, like most pink stones, soothes the emotions and eases the creative process. People with difficulties in relationships or those afraid of being hurt in matters of love will benefit from this stone and its calming influence. It also promotes the sharing of emotions.

As they have similar effects, Pink Tourmaline works well in conjunction with Rose Quartz. But in combination or alone, Pink Tourmaline will help you accept and love yourself, making it easier to be accepting of others. Pink Tourmaline helps you accept the past and work out whatever problems still exist, making you more open to new experiences.

Pink Tourmaline helps heal the body in much the same way other Tourmalines do, though it is more subtle and sensitive. It especially helps you to recognize what the problem is, where it lies, and what to do about it. You might then seek a more specific stone to focus on the problem.

Sagittarius, Libra, Leo, Aries, and Cancer have an affinity for Pink Tourmaline.

Red Tourmaline

Little is known about this stone. Some gem literature suggests using it in combination with Indocolite in order to achieve results similar to those of Watermelon Tourmaline.

Watermelon Tourmaline

Watermelon Tourmaline will benefit anyone who is drawn to it. A combination of Green and Pink Tourmaline, the Pink is usually encased in a thin layer of the Green. This stone shows us by example how opposites work together. Pink is a pale shade of red, the complementary opposite of green. Balance results from this combination.

Green Tourmaline is a problem solver; it helps us accept the past and make the present as comfortable as possible. Add to this the Pink, which makes us more loving, sensitive, and understanding in conflicts, and the result is a stone that helps us anticipate the direction a situation is going to take. Watermelon Tourmaline is a stone that teaches the lesson that only by understanding can we find true peace.

◇ ◇ ◇

Turquoise

Turquoise is a common stone that has achieved great prominence in recent years as jewelry. It ranges in color from sky blue to a soft green-blue and is found in the United States, France, and Tibet.

This stone truly reflects the individual carrying or holding it. It tunes into the energies of the person and transmits them back into the world. It can also help you get more in tune with others. Its color indicates that Turquoise is a stone that stimulates the elevation of goals or understanding. For this reason it is a popular stone with creative problem solvers. Turquoise helps us figure out how things work and where we fit in. It is meant for those who wish to communicate.

People who work as healers often wear this stone to fully understand the energy of those they are healing. Turquoise is beneficial for the entire body, but has special applications for the respiratory and immune systems. Those strongly affected by pollution will find Turquoise a helpful stone. If you are sick, Turquoise helps to put you at peace.

Mentally and spiritually, Turquoise is special in that it contains elements of both the earth, where it was formed, and the sky, which it resembles in color. Turquoise helps people realize who they are and where they are and leads them to greater self-realization.

Turquoise was common in ancient Egypt from an early period and was known to Pliny as Callais. In the thirteenth century Turquoise was said to possess the power of protecting the wearer from injury by falling (particularly from horseback). This claim was later extended to include falls from buildings over precipices.

The *Lapidaire* of Sir John Mandeville states that Turquoise protected horses from the ill effects of drinking cold water when overheated. Turks attached Turquoise to the bridles of horses as amulets, and throughout the East it was generally used as a horse amulet. It was believed to render the animals more surefooted and enduring.

A court physician of Emperor Rudolph II related a story of a Turquoise that was offered for sale after thirty years in possession of a Spaniard. The stone had entirely lost its color, but the physician's father brought it home to his son anyway, saying, "Son, as the virtues of the Turquoise are said to exist only when the stone has been given, I will try its efficacy by bestowing it upon thee." After having the stone set as a signet ring, the son wore it for a month, whereupon the stone regained its hue and splendor. Some time after that, the young man was forced to traverse a dark and dangerous road by night. His horse stumbled and threw him, but, amazingly, he was unharmed, although about a quarter of the Turquoise had broken away from the ring. On another occasion the son slipped while lifting a heavy pole and fell to his side. He heard his ribs crack, but to his surprise he discovered he was unharmed. He looked at the ring. The Turquoise had broken in two.

At the beginning of the seventeenth century, we are told, no man considered his hand to be well adorned unless he wore a fine Turquoise. Women, however, rarely wore this gem.

The Turquoise is the national stone of Persia. Some inhabitants claim that to escape evil and attain good fortune, one must see the reflection of the new moon on the face of a friend, on a copy of the Koran, or on a piece of Turquoise.

Years ago, Turquoise from the Los Cerillos mines in Mexico was crudely extracted by building large fires at the base of a rock face containing Turquoise. The natives then threw cold water onto the stone, causing it to split and shatter from the sudden temperature change. Fragmentary material was made into heart-shaped amulets called *malacates.* Mexican Indians regarded Turquoise as a sacred stone that should not pass into the possession of those who did not follow their faith.

The possession of a Turquoise was imperative for Indian medicine men who lived on the plains of North America. Without it they would not receive proper recognition. Indian legend suggests that a man who could go to the end of the rainbow and dig in the earth would find a Turquoise. If affixed to a bow, the stone was believed to help warriors or hunters become accurate marksmen.

Folklore states that if a Turquoise is offered as a pledge of friendship, the spirit dwelling in the stone is willing to transfer its offices from one person to another.

Turquoise has an affinity with all signs of the zodiac and is the common birthstone of those born in December.

Turquoise is recommended for healers, those involved in negotiations, optometrists, veterinarians, and those who must rely on communications skills to get complex ideas across.

◊ ◊ ◊

Variscite

This is a stone about which little is known. Gem literature suggests that it benefits the nervous system, the eyes, and those who wish to investigate past-life experiences. It is a green stone found in the United States.

◊ ◊ ◊

Zircon

Zircon is generally a clear stone that comes in shades of brown, red, yellow, green, and blue. It is found in North American, France, and Italy. This stone is often seen as an inexpensive look-alike for Diamond, though the healing qualities of the two stones differ greatly. Diamond amplifies the self and heightens the healing qualities of other stones. Zircon helps you reflect about your life.

Zircon helps us search out peace and quiet. Think of it as a whisper that you must concentrate on in order to hear. Zircon teaches reserve and patience.

Zircon is beneficial to the cleansing systems and improves sleep. Its use can improve your tolerance of negative situations.

Zircons are one of the birthstones assigned to persons born in December.

USING YOUR CRYSTAL OR GEMSTONE

By virtue of the fact that you're reading this book, it's clear that you are interested in the use of gemstones and crystals. What follows is a basic guide to using your crystal in many parts of your life. After you have become acquainted with the general skills that follow, you may well be able to develop your own strategies for using your crystal. Remember, always follow your intuition, and if a specific instruction feels wrong for you, don't follow it.

◊ ◊ ◊

Choosing a Crystal or Gemstone (and a Crystal or Gemstone Store)

Crystals and gemstones will come into your possession as you need them, but sometimes you will want to purchase a specific type of stone. How do you go about buying a crystal or gemstone? If you don't already know of a crystal store in your immediate area, check the phone book for listings under Crystals, Lapidaries, Minerals, or go to the nearest natural history museum. If you still have no luck, ask your local jeweler, who may sell loose, unset gems. Health food stores and alternative bookstores sometimes have information about people who sell crystals in their homes, at farmer's markets, flea markets, and craft fairs. If you have a choice of several stores, check them all out before making any decisions or purchases. As crystals rise in popularity, so do their prices. Depending on the size of the store and their stock, prices may vary greatly.

You may wonder about the relative differences between New Age crystal stores and commercial mineral stores. There are some differences in selection and in the spiritual orientation of salespeople, but never assume a crystal is better simply because it comes from a New Age store. Remember, crystals don't change you; you change yourself with the aid of the crystal. Therefore, the power of the crystal doesn't depend upon the store in which you buy it. I strongly suggest supporting smaller stores as long as prices are right, your intuitive feelings are good, and the stones you need are available. In larger urban centers some of the commercial mineral stores, like Astro Minerals in New York City, have salespeople who are well aware of the spiritual and healing qualities of gemstones and crystals and use them themselves. Rock and mineral stores generally have large stock selections and may, in fact, sell wholesale crystals to New Age crystal shops.

Let's assume you have found a store from which to buy your crystal. What's next? Take your book with you and decide exactly what you want to buy. Many stores have reference books and sheets available if you don't want to lug around a book. Ask a salesperson where the stone you're interested in is kept and take a look at what's available. Is there a particular crystal that appeals to you? If so, pick it up and get a feel for its energy. All purchases should be made intuitively. If the stone doesn't feel right to you, it isn't the best stone. Try several different stones. Does one feel better than another? If so, purchase it.

What do you do if none of them feel right? Never buy a stone you aren't sure about. Go back to the store on another occasion and try again; there may be new crystals better suited to your needs. If you have several stores to choose from and you can't find the best crystal in one, try another. Buying a crystal is an important purchase that shouldn't be forced or rushed.

Do you need to buy a crystal that's a particular size, clarity, or physical state? That's up to you. Some gem literature suggests large, perfect crystals that are, of course, quite beautiful. They can also be expensive. Once again, if a particular crystal appeals to you, don't let its price stand in your way; less perfect crystals can be just as effective and in some cases may be more suited to your energy.

In other crystals, inclusions, which may seem to be flaws, can play an important role in the use of the stone. You should be aware of this before you buy it. For the most part imperfections will not diminish the capabilities of the crystal or gemstone.

Try not to pass over beat-up-looking stones for perfectly shaped stones simply because they look better. It's the energy of the stone that's important, not its looks.

What about cut, polished, or faceted stones? Are they more suited to healing purposes? Some gem literature strongly suggests that certain gemstones or crystals be cut, faceted, or polished to intensify their healing properties. Some gem healers use primarily polished or cut stones in their healing layouts. Others feel that raw crystals directly from the earth needn't be altered. One of the primary reasons for altering the crystal or gemstone is to remove imperfections and render it more aesthetically appealing. If you feel drawn to cut or polished stones and you can afford them, by all means buy them. If you can appreciate the stone in its natural state, do not feel pressured into preferring cut or polished stones.

If you are unsure about the properties of a particular stone or wonder if you're making the right choice, don't hesitate to ask questions. If you have reservations about the country from which a gemstone originates (South Africa, for instance), don't buy the stone unless you feel you really need it. Most crystals and gemstones are mined in several countries and alternatives can be found. Most responsible crystal stores won't carry products from questionable sources. Again, if you have questions about where something comes from or whether it has been altered in some manner (for in-

stance, Smoky Quartz), just ask the salesperson. If you buy something you're not
sure about, the negative energy generated
will counter any beneficial effects you
could get from the crystal.

◇ ◇ ◇

Cleansing Your Crystal

What should you do after getting a new
crystal? First, it is best to cleanse the stone.
Do not use soap or detergent because the
cleansing is as much a spiritual ritual as
anything else. Most likely the crystals are
not dirty in a physical sense, but they do
need to be purified and attuned to the energies of the new owner.

Cleansing your crystals doesn't have to
be a complicated procedure. The most
common forms of cleansing involve put-
ting the crystal or gemstone under cold tap
water for one minute or more, soaking the
crystal in a solution of water and sea salt
for a twenty-four-hour period, or leaving the
crystal in sunlight during the peak hours
of 10 A.M. to 2 P.M. for one afternoon. Perhaps the easiest way to cleanse your crystals is to buy dried sage (either in bundles
at a gem shop or by the ounce at your local
health food store). Clarify your crystals by
burning the sage and allowing the smoke
to surround all facets of the crystal. Different experts have different means of cleansing crystals; the important thing is for you

to find a method with which you feel comfortable.

◇ ◇ ◇   *HEALING*

Getting to Know Your Crystal

Now the stone is cleansed. What should
you do with it? Read about the properties
of the stone in question in its specific entry
in this book. Does it have any properties
that will benefit you personally? Do you
want to use your stone for healing layouts,
meditation, or to improve your environment?

The first thing you should do is get to feel
comfortable with your gemstone. Examine
the stone closely, and then meditate on it
for a few minutes. If you are going to use
the stone for its healing properties, lie down
and place the stone near the area or above
the organ that needs attention. It is preferable to place the stone directly on the
skin. Concentrate on the stone, try to tune
into its energy. Then picture a current of
energy flowing from the stone directly to
the affected area. Some knowledge of anat-
omy is helpful but not essential.

Try to pick a time to do this during which
you won't be disturbed. Even fifteen minutes can be enough, though some sources
suggest thirty minutes or longer. Stones
can also be placed under your pillow during sleep. If you feel comfortable with a
particular stone, carry it with you during

stressful times. Careful analysis will tell you which stone or crystal will help you best accomplish specific goals.

Selecting Stones for Others

Choosing stones or crystals for friends is something you must be careful about. If you feel someone will greatly benefit from a particular stone, by all means give it to them. Be sure to explain the properties of the stone. Although some stones aren't dangerous, they may have certain qualities that might bring about unexpected and startling side effects, such as reawakening memories one needs to but doesn't necessarily want to deal with, or overstimulating the intestinal track during detoxification.

If you receive a stone or crystal as a gift, learn a little about it before using it yourself.

Losing a Crystal

Losing stones is a strange occurrence with which some people have difficulty. If a stone disappears, perhaps there is a reason behind it. Possession or ownership is a concept that has become an obsession in Western civilization. In many ancient cultures, indeed, even today in some remote countries, ownership is not recognized as a realistic or rational idea. Members of these civilizations believe that all things belong to everyone; individuals are willing to share with everybody else during hard times. These societies also believe that if something disappears, it probably wasn't meant to be in your possession at that point anyway. Perhaps people lose things to learn how to deal with less, or objects fall into someone else's possession because the other person is in greater need of the object. Never assume that an object is so important that its loss will ruin your life in some way. If you need it, it may reappear or a new stone may come into your possession.

◊ ◊ ◊

Placing Your Crystals

Placing stones or crystals about your personal environment is an important matter. Because the vibrational energy is a constant in the rock's existence, you need to decide where you want all that energy to go. Certain stones, such as Rose Quartz, can be placed in any environment without question; their influence is completely tuned to bringing about happiness and love. Red or orange stones may be too stimulating to have a consistently positive effect upon a room. If you think you need extra stimulation for a while, always be sure to move the stones when the period has passed.

Crystals should be placed according to your intuition, whether at home, in sleeping areas, in the workplace, or about your body. It is a good idea to keep all crystals away from electrical appliances or machinery. An exception to this rule is color TV sets, upon which a crystal may be placed to absorb radiation.

At the Office

Crystals that relate to business should be kept in the workplace and not transferred to living areas. Check specific entries according to career vocation. Good crystals for the workplace are Rose Quartz (helps people get along with others), Emeralds (aids in working in close quarters), Jasper (gives stamina and endurance), crystal clusters (facilitates living and working with others in a harmonious manner), Clear Quartz (equalizes energy), Jade (relaxes the mind), and Fluorite (helps mental activity). Other specific crystals are recommended for certain people: square-cut Garnets are good for business people; Tourmalines are excellent for counselors; Crysocola and other blue stones are help for artists; many of the Agates are recommended for public speakers, teachers, lecturers, and those who have to communicate complicated ideas in a simple manner. Workplace crystals can be placed on top of desks, on bookcase shelves, on windowsills, or even in the soil of ailing plants. If possible, crystals should get some exposure to sun throughout the day, and be cleansed after upsetting office occurrences in order to clear the crystals of any negative energy that they may have absorbed. However, this should not become a ritualized procedure. Crystals will transmit energy whether or not we are aware of them doing so; it is a natural process that they perform. Let intuition and instinct guide you in your crystal use. They should be used in an attitude of play and discovery rather than seriously considered as a panacea for all of life's problems and stressful situations. The only thing you *must* do is treat them with respect.

At Home

Crystals and gemstones can be placed around the home to channel energy constructively throughout your living quarters. Crystal clusters and formations can be used as decorative items on coffee tables, bathtubs (one at each corner of the tub), kitchen counters, home workplaces, and sleeping areas. Crystal prisms can be hung from windows to send rays of color throughout the room when the window is getting sunlight. Crystals are highly effective placed on windowsills where they can get daily exposure to the sun. You can balance out the energy of any room if Quartz crystals are placed around the room with points directed north and west.

Recommended gemstones for the home are Turquoise, which protects against environmental pollutants; all varieties of Coral (except Black); Jade for its soothing qualities; Amber for its protective nature; Rose Quartz for love, tenderness, gentleness, and its ability to create a warm environment in which you can feel loved. Fluorite (dispels psychic clutter), is also a good choice, as are Black Tourmaline (repels negative energy), Malachite (if you live near a nuclear power plant), Malachite/Azurite (to soothe and calm the spirit), and Lapis Lazuli. Topaz is recommended for home use because it relaxes while enhancing creativity, and Smoky Quartz because it increases creativity, fertility, and joy.

Sleeping Areas

Sleeping areas should be treated separately. Much of the work of the subconscious occurs during dreaming, and tissue regeneration is at its peak during REM states. Because of the highly intimate nature of dreaming and sleeping, your most personal stones can be kept effectively by the bedside. The gemstones will be those that you know instinctively belong specifically to you. You probably will not want others to handle them. Aside from your personal stones, effective stones to keep on a table or windowsill by sleeping areas are: Herkimer Diamonds, which aid in dream work; Amethysts for their ability to assist spiritual and psychic opening in a grounded way and for their positive effect on the nervous system; Rutilated Quartz because of its ability to spur tissue regeneration.

Body Work

Gemstones and crystals are used in healing layouts to align the energy within the physical body. There are several points along the body that have been traditionally used in healing and correspond to the endocrine glands. These points are the crown of the head, a point in the middle of the forehead, the base of the throat, the midpoint of the chest just over the heart, the solar plexus, the midpoint of the abdomen three fingers below the navel, and the pubic bone. There are several similar exercises that can be performed to relax a person and help them attain a sense of well-being and physical integrity.

Meditation Exercises

Exercise 1

Lie on your back in a comfortable, darkened room free from drafts. If it helps you to relax, play some meditation music and light a colored candle. Holding a clear crystal with which you feel a special tie or affinity, move the crystal over your body, positioning it over each body point described above for about fifteen minutes. Hold the base of the crystal toward you.

Move the crystal about in a gradual and relaxed manner. Breath slowly, concentrating on breathing from the belly rather than the upper part of the chest. Visualize white healing light coming in from the crystal point on the inhale, and all the tension and stress passing out of the crystal on the exhale.

When you have finished, lie quietly and notice the changes that have occurred in your body.

At first you may want to spend less than fifteen minutes on each area of the body.

Exercise 2

This exercise requires eleven Clear Quartz crystals of about the same size. Use single-terminated crystals, not crystals with points on each end.

Lie in a comfortable darkened area, light your favorite candle, and turn on your meditation music. Place a crystal on the floor at the top of your head, one on your forehead, one on your throat, chest, solar plexus, abdomen, and pubic bone. All crystals should be laid lengthwise on the body with the tips pointed up. Place a crystal in the palm of each hand and breathe slowly and deeply from the abdomen, visualizing healing energy flowing into your body as all tension and stress flows out through the crystals.

Exercise 3

This meditation exercise incorporates gemstones by color gradation. You can add or subtract gemstones as you feel the need; the ones recommended are not necessarily the only ones that can or should be used. However, make sure you check body placement of stones in earlier entries of this book so that you are not working against a crystal's influence. In this exercise you are using stones according to their color, arranging them on your body as colors appear when white light is refracted in a prism or rainbow.

Place a Smoky Quartz on your pelvic bone; Bloodstone, Garnet, or Ruby on your abdomen; Citrine or Topaz on your navel; Peridot or Green Tourmaline on your solar plexus; Rose Quartz or Rhodochrosite on your heart; Turquoise or Chrysocolla at your throat; Amethyst or Azurite in the middle of your forehead; and a Clear Quartz crystal at the crown of your head. Place a Clear Quartz crystal in each palm and instep of each foot.

Lie quietly on the floor for fifteen to thirty minutes, relaxing and breathing deeply from your abdomen. When you are finished, remove the stones slowly and concentrate on what impressions you received.

◇ ◇ ◇

Mini-Exercises for Quick Stress Relief

Often during the course of a day, stress builds up to the point where it is damaging. Yet since most of us work outside the home or lack the necessary solitude to perform more elaborate exercises with crystals, we simply do not get the time or the chance to take advantage of the crystal's powers during an ordinary day. When you find yourself in a pressurized situation, here are some mini-exercises to help relieve stress and regain your perspective.

1. Many stressful situations result simply from the fact that we are often unable to express ourselves and our feelings. When faced with a stressful situation where you want to be more assertive yet find yourself afraid or unable to say what's on your mind, take a moment to concentrate on aligning your body's energies, and lightly press a piece of Turquoise or Aquamarine against your throat. This exercise frees the voice, and in turn you will find yourself able to clearly and naturally express what you have been unable or afraid to say. Remember, though, these stones rule the use of the spoken word to express truth. They will not work if you are using their energy in anger or deception.

2. Faced with a decision and you can't find the answer? Try this: sit or stand straight to align your energy, and while looking out the window or at some point of concentration, fill your mind with white light. Then, to open your intuitive channels and allow your subconscious knowledge to provide you with the correct choice, place a piece of Lapis Lazuli or Azurite over your third eye. Listen to your inner voice, breathe deeply, and do not allow worry or confusion to intrude upon the light of illumination now filling your thoughts. Before long, you will have an answer.

3. Just got laid off? And in less than an hour, somebody tried to snatch your wallet, spilled coffee on your brand-new $1,500 designer coat, and the subway broke down, leaving you stranded in the tunnel with five hundred brand-new close friends, several of whom have not bathed in the last few years? For those days when it's been more than you can stand, try this. Find a point of concentration, take a deep breath, and press the first three fingers of your left hand lightly on your abdomen just beneath your navel. Center your attention on this point; concentrate on all the tension leaving your arms and legs. Fill this point with white light and draw the light into yourself. Recommended for situations like this are Jasper, Bloodstone, Carnelian, or Garnet. If you don't have

the stones at hand, don't worry. As you draw the white-light energy into yourself, concentrate on visualizing these stones. Then, when you have the opportunity, take them out and repeat the exercise to reinforce the grounding and stress-relieving procedures.

Pets and Crystals

Many people have pets that play an important role in their lives. To some it will seem natural to share their energy, amplified through crystals, with the pet.

Pets are a natural part of our world. They are friends that depend upon us for food and shelter and emotional support. They return that support quite readily. Much research has been conducted on the psychology of animals, but you don't need a book to recognize your pets' emotional states. Unlike humans, they usually let you know what's on their minds. And if you're sad, your dog may lick your tears away. It is amazing how tuned into your emotions your pet is.

If you are introducing crystals into your life and you have a pet, think about what effect the crystal may have on it. If your life improves, most likely its life improves. The most obvious way of affecting both your lives is through crystal placement around your living environment.

A Crystal Just for Your Pet

Does your pet have a special area to which it is restricted? Consider placing a piece of Rose Quartz nearby as a soothing influence. Is it hyperactive or lethargic? Try placing a Carnelian for stimulation, or Amethyst for a tranquil influence, near the sleeping area. Do you have a bird that won't sing? Try placing Amazonite or Rhodonite somewhere in or near the cage.

Although it is difficult to prove that the crystals are bringing about major changes in the quality of your pet's life, they can certainly be considered a benign and positive influence. However, you should use some caution when placing the stone. Animals usually show curiosity about any new object. *Do not let the animal swallow the crystal.* To avoid this possibility, make sure the crystal is either too large for this to happen, or that it is in a place where the animal can't reach it. A nice suggestion for pets with collars is a small pendant that can be attached to the buckle. If the pet has a bed or box to sleep in, try taping the stone to the bottom, out of the animal's view.

If you wish to try a healing layout with your animal, do this with great caution. Animals have a very different anatomical structure from humans and should not be treated as a human would be. Also, consider that most animals find it difficult to stay in one place for such a treatment.

Crystals and the New Pet

When you bring a new pet home, have a few stones that will help it adjust to and accept its new environment. Some suggestions are Rose Quartz, Pyrite, Lazulite, or Picture Agate. Singularly or in combination, these stones can soothe and help make an environment more comfortable. Think of it as a New Age alternative to supplying a new puppy with a ticking clock.

Do not be alarmed if your pet licks or plays with a stone. If the stones have been properly cleansed, the stone presents no danger. Animals base many of their judgments upon instincts. If they seem attracted to a particular stone, there is something about the stone they can relate to on some level.

The Erotic Crystal

Just as crystals can be used in other areas of your life, you can use their power to enhance and encourage sexual expression and erotic pleasure. Crystal power will not solve every problem you encounter in your sex life, but it can certainly help overcome some of the stumbling blocks to true erotic enjoyment.

Enhancing Your Pleasure

Many people feel that sex is the one area of their lives that is beyond control; attraction, sexual fulfillment, and even love all remain mysterious and indefinable chemistry. To some extent, of course, this is true, but on the other hand, those are the very qualities that make sex and sexual attraction as mysterious and exciting as they are. One thing almost everyone does agree on, though, is that in order to fully experience sexual love, you must first love yourself. Any sexual experience can only be hampered by feelings of unworthiness, unattractiveness, or inadequacy. Therefore, the first step in finding sexual appreciation and fulfillment is in learning to appreciate yourself.

Perfume a warm bath with rose oil and a few grains of sea salt. Drop an Emerald into the water. Soak for at least a half an hour, cleansing your aura and allowing yourself to experience some pleasurable fantasies. See yourself as the beautiful and desirable being that you truly are. Nurture this feeling of self-love as carefully as you would nurture someone else's love for you. To keep these feelings with you throughout the day or night, carry Rose Quartz, Carnelian, and Rhodochrosite.

If you have trouble transforming your feelings into physical action, you might want to wear a pendant in the center of your chest. Stones that are best for this charm are Green Tourmaline and Kunzite.

For those who have trouble sharing physical pleasure, Pink Tourmaline is recommended.

Assuming that you already have met, or meet, someone with whom you might enjoy a sexual encounter, there is no guarantee that he or she will share your enthusiasm for crystal therapy, particularly in the heat of the moment! Many of the old rituals prescribed for increased sexual pleasure through the use of crystals are far too complicated and, in some instances, inhibit spontaneity. Nonetheless, you can create a subtle aphrodisiac effect by scattering a few Carnelians or Pink Tourmalines on your bedside table or nightstand. Should you prefer passion on the living room carpet, the coffee table will do nicely!

Sexual pleasure can be prolonged by wearing a small piece of Jasper in an earring or necklace. Set in gold, Jasper's aphrodisiac effects are greatly enhanced.

Enhancing Your Partner's Pleasure

Too often, poor sexual relations is the result of poor communication between partners. Should you find yourself in such a situation, try this:

Lie together side by side, preferably in the nude. Place a Garnet over the third eye of one partner for three to five minutes. Lie together in silence, enjoying each other's closeness and warmth. When the time has passed, have the first partner place the Garnet on the other's third eye and repeat and enjoy those few minutes of closeness and quiet. After the exercise is completed, even the most difficult or embarrassing topics will prove easier to broach and discuss in calm and harmony.

For fertility, Smoky Quartz, Carnelian, Chrysocolla, Chrysoprase, Jet, and Black Quartz carried throughout the months make the body most receptive to reproduction. On the male side, Jet and Black Quartz have been reported to increase virility and sexual stamina.

Storing Crystals

Crystals will pass in and out of your life as you need them at specific times. Different people use different systems when working with crystals. Experiment with your crystals until you find the system that's right for you. But use your crystals carefully and don't try to rush your progress or growth. Crystals and gemstones are meant to be aids in development; each person has his or her own specific needs.

When carrying crystals on the body or moving them from place to place, keep them in a soft pouch to protect them from cracking, chipping, or altering the energy that they may pick up from being exposed to environmental influences. By simply placing crystals in sunlight for two hours, you can recharge them. Small groups of crystals can be buried in earth, or if you want to keep them stored for longer periods of time, wrap them in a natural fabric and bury them in a box in the ground. When you are ready to use them again, unwrap them and place in direct sunlight.

If you wish to cleanse or temporarily recharge a crystal, you can bury it in sea salt. Do not be upset if you lose your crystals; they will reappear when you need them or travel to a new owner who has greater need of them than you. And do not be afraid to give them away to people, especially if someone exhibits a special fascination or attraction to a crystal you own. Obviously, if the crystal holds deeply personal feelings for you as well, don't give it away. In fact, a good solution would be to offer to loan the crystal out for, say, a week. You might be pleasantly surprised to find that after living without the favorite crystal for a few days, it was time to give it up and move on.

SPENDING
A DAY
WITH YOUR
CRYSTALS

Set apart a crystal day, in which you won't be disturbed, devoted to letting your crystals work for you. You will be surprised at the insights and freedom that you experience even in the middle of stressful existence. This suggested program can be followed alone or with a friend. Feel free to add or improvise as you go along. One day a month with your crystals when the moon is waxing will provide surprising insights into your personality and problem-solving capabilities.

This program can be followed anywhere you can create a relaxing environment. Even the busiest of cities have parks and inspirational environments from which you can draw energy that can revitalize you and put you at peace. Don't worry about bad weather; violent rainstorms have unique creative energy, and everyone has experienced peaceful self-discovery during an unexpected snowy day. If you plan to do crystal work on a day in which bad weather occurs, perhaps you needed that particular boost of energy in your life.

1. The Night Before

Before going to bed, burn some sage around your living space. Concentrate on areas that have been the location of unease, anger, arguments, or depression. Concentrate also on your sleeping areas.

Arrange your sleeping crystals around your bed. If you sleep under a window, you might want to set a row of Quartz crystals on your windowsill. Play with the arrangement. Good crystals to put by your bedside are those with which you feel a strong personal attachment, as well as clear crystals, Smoky Quartz, and Amethyst. If you have trouble sleeping due to nervous tension, shells, fossil, and Agate will help.

Place a candle by your bed. This should be secured and encased in a glass chimney so it won't fall over in the night—you are going to let the candle burn while you sleep. Good colors for your candle are white, purple, or dark blue. Stay away from orange or red colors, since these can be too stimulating.

Now you are ready for your bath. Run a slightly warm bath in which you place several tablespoons of baking soda. If you like, you can place Quartz crystals at each corner of the bathtub, points facing toward you. Place a piece of Pink Quartz, Rhodochrosite, Moonstone, or Pearl on or near the bathtub where you can see it clearly.

You will also need a pink or white candle. Turn out the lights, light the candle, and concentrate on feeling loved and in tune with your emotions. Pink Quartz, Rhodochrosite, and Pearl aid in developing feelings of self-love; Pearl and Moonstone are nurturing.

Now relax. Let all the tension float out of your body. When you are completely relaxed, visualize a ball of white light surrounding you, through which nothing of a disturbing nature can enter. Let images float into your mind and let them go. See yourself surrounded by gently pulsing, nurturing energy.

Look at the crystal or crystals you have chosen to bring into your bathing area and concentrate on them, visualizing them as loving protectors. Breathe slowly and deeply and let whatever thoughts and feelings you may have rise to the surface. Focus on a particular feeling or problem that interests you and tell yourself to remember to dream about this during the night.

Your bath should take twenty to thirty minutes. You can adjust the water temperature to make yourself comfortable.

When you are finished, dry off and put on soft, familiar sleeping clothes in a color that makes you happy. Try to avoid dark browns, blacks, and dirty beige. Blue, pink, gentle greens, soft yellows, and violets are good. So is white if it is not too harsh.

Get into bed. You will need three Quartz crystals. Lie on your back and place one crystal in the middle of your forehead and

one in the palm of each hand. Visualize
yourself filled with a calm white energy
that pours into you through the crystals.
After about ten minutes, set your clock to
one half hour before you usually get up in
the morning and go to sleep, reminding
yourself to dream through the thoughts
that rose in your mind earlier in the bathtub.

2. First Thing in the Morning

Wake up slowly and lie in bed for a few
minutes, concentrating on what happened
in your sleep. Try to remember any dreams
or thoughts you might have had and make
notes. These problems or insights may be
things to which you will want to return
later on in the day. When you are satisfied
that you have reviewed your dream activity, sit up slowly in bed and hold a clear
crystal to your solar plexus. This will help
you to feel grounded and ready to start the
day. Drink a glass of water with the juice
of half a lemon squeezed into it and do your
favorite stretching exercises. Now you are
ready to go outside. You can take either a
brisk walk or a run in a natural environment. Take along clear Quartz crystals and
Herkimer Diamonds. They will give you
energy and boost your morale. If you are a
nature lover, you might want to also carry
pieces of Diopside, Enstatite, Petrified

Wood, or Amethyst. It is not necessary to load yourself down with crystals; just pick one or two that appeal to you in a special way.

Spend at least thirty minutes to an hour outside. After running or walking you can do tai chi, yoga, or simply sit in a quiet area meditating on the crystal or crystals that you have brought with you.

Be open to the things happening around you. Remember, this is a day for experiencing new things in peace and tranquility.

◊ ◊ ◊

3. Mid Morning

After breakfast, which should be a healthy meal of fruit and grain, devote yourself to creative activity. Write a poem, play music, draw a picture, do needlework, or read an inspirational book. Play with your pets or children. Stones that you might like to have surrounding you are Kunzite, Sapphire, Garnet, and Chrysolite.

◊ ◊ ◊

4. Noon

At noon, take four Quartz crystals and a Diamond or Herkimer Diamond outside with you. Arrange the Quartz around you, points facing in. Place the Diamond, or

Herkimer Diamond, crystal in front of you where it can be easily seen. Sit comfortably and relax. Breathing from your abdomen in slow, even breaths, concentrate on the crystal in front of you. Imagine yourself inside the crystal, surrounded by its protection and beauty. Be aware that any crystal is a concentration of structures working together. See yourself as a facet of the crystal. Meditate on your crystal, letting it tell you what you need to know. When you are finished, sit quietly for a few moments reflecting on what you have learned.

5. Afternoon

After a light lunch of salad or stir-fried vegetables, you can try your hand at crystal gazing. For a more extensive explanation of this activity, consult the chapter on crystal gazing.

Arrange your crystal on a table in front of which you can sit comfortably. A crystal ball is not necessary. Any quartz crystal will do, especially a window crystal or channeling crystal. You can also use fisherman's floats as well as blue or green spheres (be sure to cleanse them before you use them for crystal gazing). Many crystal gazers swear by the relatively inexpensive lucite balls that you can find in New Age bookstores and occult shops. You may find to your surprise that images develop from either darkened or light points in the glass.

Relax and concentrate on the problem at hand. Perhaps you want to clarify your feelings about an emotional problem or understand how best to handle a particularly sticky business situation.

Think through all your options in a clear and concise way. If you find yourself getting muddled or confused, perhaps you are asking the wrong questions and need to go back and reconsider what it is that you really want to know. Once you have centered on a particular area of concentration, relax once more and stare into your crystal. If you have problems focusing, be patient and remember that crystal gazing is not an area in which your performance matters; it is only an aid to free your subconscious. Results will come in time. Relax and start again.

At first you may be surprised at what you see. Often the images that arise in the mind are similar to the things some people see before going to sleep at night. You may see the faces of your friends or even people with whom you are unfamiliar. This is nothing to wonder about, just concentrate on specific qualities present in the person. They are reflected there by your subconscious in an attempt to teach you something specific, and working as keys to unlock information to which you already have the answer. Perhaps you will see objects or places that have special importance to you. Follow carefully what appears

on the crystal and when the images flicker
out, sit quietly for several minutes and reflect on what has occurred. Good stones to
have surrounding you when you are doing
this exercise are Turquoise, which aids in
mental relaxation; Amethyst, which fosters intuition; Chrysocolla, which strengthens inner perception; Zircon; blue and
white Quartz; and Azurite, for improving
your psychic ability.

You might want to try your crystal gazing in a darkened room with soft music
playing in the background to increase your
concentration.

What if you don't like what you see in
your crystal ball? If you sense that the images coming through your crystal ball are
negative, alien, or just plain silly, chances
are a) your concentration is not centered
properly; or b) the specific crystal you are
using may contain negative energies associated with prior owners. Your own intuition will tell you whether or not you are
getting images that are yours. If you sense
that these images are not constructive, take
a break, clear your crystal by burying it in
sea salt, and go back to it another time.

6. Evening

Pamper yourself with a healthy dinner
served in relaxed and beautiful surroundings. Eat by candlelight with soft music

playing in the background. You can even have a few friends over who are sympathetic to what you have been doing. It might be fun to see a friend or two who has also been spending the day with his or her crystals.

When you are finished, go outside for a walk. Think about what has been happening throughout the day. If you do tai chi or yoga, you can do a half-hour session outside. When you are finished, sit and calmly reflect on your life. Establish one or two goals for yourself that you can achieve easily. Think about where you are going and what characteristics you would like to develop in yourself.

After your friends leave, sit in a darkened room with clear Quartz crystals surrounding you. Before you, on the floor or table, arrange a circle of gemstones according to color. Place a Diamond or clear crystal in the middle and a green stone above the crystal facing you. Moving around the Diamond in a circle from left to right, place a red stone, orange stone, yellow stone, green stone, blue stone, indigo stone, and violet stone. Check the charts in the back of this book to find stones listed under the various colors and pick stones with which you have a particular affinity.

Light a candle and place it where you can see it easily. Stare at the candle flame for two minutes after you have relaxed and regulated your breath. Then place your hands over your eyes and concentrate on maintaining the image of the candle before you. This will help you concentrate on the quality of the stones that surround you.

Begin by picturing yourself surrounded by a field of white light. When you feel comfortable, inhale the light into your body. Sense it filling every part of you, shining out from your eyes.

Beginning with the red stones, feel the waves of color enveloping you. Red stones contribute tremendous animal energy analogous to fire and creation. Orange stones relate to your abdomen and transform the fire energy to the power source of your solar plexus, identified by the color yellow. Draw the energy of the yellow stones into your solar plexus. Draw the green color of the stones opposite you into your heart to enable you to feel love and compassion for living things. The color blue from the stones before you can then be drawn into your throat, helping you communicate your ideas more clearly. Draw the indigo color from the indigo stones before you into the center of your forehead. This will help attune you to higher truth. Finally, draw the violet color from the violet stones into the crown of your head and let everything around you become a part of your experience.

Concentrate on visualizing yourself as a rainbow full of color shining in joy toward the world.

BIRTHSTONES

The idea that certain precious and semi-precious stones correspond to the months of the year or the twelve signs of the zodiac is a very old one dating back to the fifth century. References to birthstones (or natal stones) are found in the Bible in the book of Revelation (21:18). The first stone, a Jasper, is assigned to St. Peter and corresponds with the month of March and the vernal equinox. Thus, the earliest birthstones had three distinct historical associations—the months of the year, the signs of the zodiac, and the twelve apostles.

Yet the wearing of natal stones did not come into common practice until well into the eighteenth century, in Eastern Europe. Natal stones were worn initially as talismans, particular charms against disease, or as aids in bringing about the wearer's wishes. Early wearers of stones relied heavily on a belief in the powers of a particular stone. The correspondence between an individual stone's vibrations and natal signs was not widely accepted until much later. Initially, at least, most people who wore natal stones probably owned a set of twelve, changing them as the months passed. As gemstones became more accessible through traveling dealers and tradesmen, the custom spread beyond Eastern Europe.

Interestingly enough, however, there developed surprisingly little variation from the twelve stones first assigned in the book of Revelation as the foundation stones, or those associated with the twelve apostles. Whether these stones are assigned to signs of the zodiac or months of the year, traditions in any number of countries correspond roughly to the same twelve stones, as though there were some hidden, yet overwhelming, consensus as to the properties of certain stones. For example, in the fifteenth century, Jews, Romans, Arabians, Russians, and Italians all held the Garnet to be the overwhelming favorite gemstone for the month of January.

That is why it is best to defer to traditional ideas in purchasing natal birthstones. The instinct and practice of centuries tells us that particular stones do, in fact, give off vibrations that correspond to months and signs of the zodiac, and despite the attempts of commercial concerns to change these designations, sooner or later we always return to them.

Following is a list of these birthstones, including (where appropriate and acceptable) some alternate stones:

January	Garnet	
February	Amethyst	
March	Bloodstone	(Aquamarine)
April	Diamond	
May	Emerald	
June	Pearl	
July	Turquoise	

August	Sardonyx	
September	Peridot	
October	Beryl	(Tourmaline)
November	Topaz	
December	Ruby	(Lapis Lazuli)

Though there is a powerful tradition associated with wearing birthstones, you can add to your definition of appropriate stones by adding to the month stone those stones that correspond to your sign of the zodiac or the season of the year. Some find it preferable to have a particular piece of jewelry including all their appropriate birthstones and wear this ornament as a powerful personal talisman.

Season	Stone
Spring	Emerald
Summer	Ruby
Autumn	Sapphire
Winter	Diamond

Zodiac Sign:	Stone
Aries	Diamond
Taurus	Emerald
Gemini	Moss Agate *or* Pearl
Cancer	Moonstone
Leo	Onyx *or* Smoky Quartz
Virgo	Sapphire
Libra	Opal *or* Tourmaline
Scorpio	Topaz
Sagittarius	Lapis Lazuli
Capricorn	Ruby
Aquarius	Aquamarine
Pisces	Amethyst

Many of the stones associated with seasons and signs are based not only on their obvious associations—Emerald for the green months of spring, for example—but also on their planetary rulers. Emerald rules the green of spring but is also chosen for its association with the planet Venus, which in turn rules Taurus, a spring sign. Moonstone, associated with the Moon-ruled sign of Cancer, is also chosen because of its wavery light-refracting qualities, not unlike moonlight or the haziness of a summer afternoon.

Keep the special qualities of each stone in mind when choosing your combinations of birthstones, and keep in mind, too, those particular stones that evoke the best response in you. Also, if you are aware of a particular concentration of planets in one area of your astrological chart, you may feel drawn to stones other than your birthstone in constructing your personal talismans. For example, a Leo with a high concentration of the air sign Gemini in his or her chart may not truly respond to Onyx but feel more drawn to a Moss Agate or Pearl. Used in combination with the summer stone Ruby and the alternate Smoky Topaz, Gemini stones will form a spiritually compatible complement to the fiery summer stones.

Another way to add to your repertory of birthstones is to wear your individual birthstone in combination with the stone ruling the current month of the year—a Ruby in December, a Garnet in January.

Some gem literature states that when worn in this fashion, birthstones supply both protection and the needed energy boosts necessary to deal with different planetary vibrations and environmental occurrences specific to certain times of the year. Keep in mind that the stones need not be worn as jewelry or talismans, but that a small chip or piece of stone will be sufficient when carried with you at all times. Be sure also that your individual birthstone is compatible with a specific month's stone, and if you find that it is not, use an alternate. Check specific entries elsewhere in this book for gem affinities.

CRYSTAL
GAZING

Since the beginning of time, mankind has used reflective surfaces in an attempt to know the future. Perhaps the first scryer gazed into a water pot to find images forming there. Scryers used whatever they found around them: polished steel, lead droplets, mirrors, quicksilver, even pools of ink. Modern diviners often use fisherman's floats and many New Age stores sell lucite crystal balls.

Crystal balls became prominent in the Middle Ages and were cherished and passed down to apprentices by their masters. The points of light that reflect from the polished surface fix the eye of the gazer until the optic nerve gradually ceases to transmit outside stimuli. It then begins to respond to the reflex action proceeding from the brain of the gazer. In this way internal impressions are projected externally and only seem to come from the outside. Sometimes prolonged gazing can cause temporary loss of sight; the optic nerve becomes paralyzed to external impression, able only to reflect internal stimulus from the brain center. People who practice crystal divination almost invariably state that the crystal seems to disappear and a mist rises before their eyes before images flicker to the surface.

As scrying developed, its practitioners

settled on polished spheres of Beryl, and later on crystal balls. Rock crystal was decreed the best material for the purpose. Druids apparently used Beryl for scrying, the Scottish Highlanders termed these objects "stones of power."

Paracelsus declares in his writing on conjuring crystals that "to conjure" means nothing more than to "observe anything rightly, to learn and understand what it is."

Elaborate rituals were used by ancients in consecrating crystal balls, involving incantations, burying the objects in graves, and careful attention to planetary positions during manufacture. Often young children were used to read the crystal. Wealthy people employed scryers in their household as they did physicians. Dr. Dee, a prominent figure at the court of Emperor Rudolf II, was also highly favored by Queen Elizabeth I, who visited him several times and consulted him on political matters.

Most of the early records of crystal gazing show conclusively enough that the images revealed in the stone were produced by the expectations, hopes, or fears of the gazer. In many cases the visions were prophetic solely because they determined the future conduct of the person who consulted the stone. Persuaded that what he or she had seen must come to pass, the gazer proceeded to make the vision come true.

The advantage of using a ball in which to scry is that it multiplies reflections and light points so the sight is induced to wander from point to point, thereby suggesting forms and motions by the combination of the numerous reflections. Often, too, a light point visible to one eye will not be so to the other, provoking the phenomenon of binocular vision that will exist for a moment or two when the diverse images coalesce again, giving an impression of movement. For an individual gifted with imagination and the natural quality of visualizing brain pictures (similar to the phenomenon of images appearing before the eyes just before sleep), shifting light points and repeated reflections of surrounding objects offer a great deal of material out of which to construct the lifelike visions viewed in a crystal. Whether these pictures have specific psychic power other than their value as phenomena depends upon the significance we attribute to the process of the subconscious. Certainly it is true that the narrow limits of day-to-day personality are sometimes transcended.

In England, all those who attempted to reveal the hidden secrets of the future were expressly designated as rogues and vagabonds according to the terms of an act passed in 1824. Such offenders, on being duly convicted before the Justice of the Peace, could be committed to a house of correction, "there to be kept at hard labor for any time not exceeding three calendar months." This class of undesirables comprised all those using subtle craft of divination for the deception of His Majesty's subjects.

The diviners of the Yucatan placed great

reliance on "clear stones." These may have been Quartz crystals or other translucent stones, but to serve for divining purposes the stones were sanctified according to special rites; gum copal was burned before them as magic formulas transmitted from generation to generation were recited. When cleansed, the diviner claimed to see the whereabouts of lost articles as well as activities of absent persons.

Apache medicine men used crystals for inducing visions and regaining lost property, particularly recovering stolen ponies.

Australians and natives of New Guinea made amulets of leather and Quartz crystals that were then used for rainmaking. Crystal balls have been found in graves, tombs, and funeral urns all over the world.

A turn-of-the-century instruction in crystal gazing suggested placing the crystal on a table. A velvet screen was set up to protect it from the reflections of surrounding objects. Seven candlesticks with wax tapers were arranged in front of the screen. The tapers were then to be lighted, the room being otherwise in perfect darkness, and the would-be scryer was advised to seat himself comfortably before the table, lay his hands flat upon it, and gaze fixedly upon the crystal for half an hour or longer. Apparently the light from the tapers would then produce a multitude of light points in the crystal. In order to maintain psychic contact with the crystal ball, the gazer was advised to put the crystal ball beneath his pillow when retiring to rest.

The crystal gazer was strongly advised by some to limit the duration of his experiment at first to five minutes, during which he was to avoid thinking of anything in particular while keeping his eyes fixed intently upon the ball, without any undue straining of attention. Should his eyes water after the test was concluded, this indicated that the gazer had persisted too long. Even after considerable practice, we are told scrying should not be carried on for more than a few minutes at a time.

For hundreds of years crystal balls were tediously made by hand in Japan. The mass of crystal was chipped with a small steel hammer to form a sphere. It was then given to a grinder who placed the ball inside a cast-iron cylinder along with fragments of emery and garnet. The cylinder was turned constantly for several days while water washed through it, lubricating the crystal as it was ground smooth. The final polishing was done with ground hematite. Germany, France, and the United States produced crystal balls by machinery, holding the crystal against a turning grindstone while constantly washing it with water. It was apparently an unhealthy profession, since many of the men who ground these balls died of consumption.

CHARTS
FOR
INSTANT
REFERENCE

ZODIAC AFFINITIES

AQUARIUS

Aquamarine
Chrysoprase
Garnet
Labradorite
Lapis Lazuli
Opal

PISCES

Albite
Amethyst
Aquamarine
Chrysoprase
Fluorite
Green
Tourmaline
Labradorite
Moonstone
Opal

ARIES

Amethyst
Carnelian
Fire Agate
Garnet
Pink
Tourmaline
Topaz

TAURUS

Aquamarine
Emerald
Kunzite
Lapis Lazuli
Rose Quartz
Sapphire

GEMINI

Agate
Chrysocolla
Chrysoprase
Sapphire
Topaz

CANCER

Albite
Chrysoprase
Emerald
Green
Tourmaline
Moonstone
Opal
Pink
Tourmaline
Rhodochro-
site

LEO

Amber
Carnelian
Chrysocolla

VIRGO

Amazonite
Amber
Carnelian

LIBRA

Aquamarine
Emerald
Kunzite

LEO	*VIRGO*	*LIBRA*
Citrine	Chrysocolla	Moonstone
Fire Agate	Citrine	Opal
Garnet	Sapphire	Peridot
Pink		Pink
Tourmaline		Tourmaline
Ruby		Sapphire
Topaz		

SCORPIO	*SAGITTARIUS*	*CAPRICORN*
Albite	Amethyst	Amber
Aquamarine	Azurite	Amethyst
Emerald	Labradorite	Carnelian
Garnet	Lapis Lazuli	Fire Agate
Green	Pink	Garnet
Tourmaline	Tourmaline	Green
Malachite	Ruby	Tourmaline
Moonstone	Sodalite	Labradorite
Obsidian	Topaz	Peridot
Ruby		Ruby
		Sapphire

STONES FOR ANY SIGN

Bloodstone
Coral
Diamond
Jade
Malachite/Azurite
Pearl
Clear Quartz
Rose Quartz
Smoky Quartz
Turquoise
Watermelon Tourmaline

STONES AND THEIR SIGNS BY COLOR

Red	Aries, Scorpio	Bloodstone, Coral, Garnet, Ruby
Pink		Kunzite, Rhodochrosite, Rubelite, Watermelon Tourmaline
Orange	Leo	Carnelian, Fire Opal
Yellow	Libra, Taurus	Amber, Citrine, Topaz
Green	Cancer	Emerald, Jade, Malachite, Tourmaline
Blue	Capricorn	Aquamarine, Chrysocolla, Lapis Lazuli, Sapphire, Turquoise
Indigo	Aquarius, Pisces	Azurite
Violet	Gemini, Virgo	Amethyst
Purple	Sagittarius	Purple Fluorite
White		Diamond, Moonstone, Pearl, Clear Quartz
Black		Jet, Obsidian, Black Tourmaline

WHERE TO WEAR CRYSTALS

Agate, Fire	forehead
Amber	wrist
Apatite	earlobes, thumb
Bloodstone	earlobes, throat
Chalcedony	heart
Chrysolite	throat
Copper	anywhere, forehead
Coral	forehead
Diamond	finger, temple
Emerald	heart, ring finger, right arm
Fluorite	earlobes
Garnet	earlobes, heart
Gold	anywhere
Granite	throat
Hematite	base of spine
Herkimer Diamond	base of spine
Jade	anywhere
Jasper, Green	anywhere
Jasper, Picture	earlobes, heart, throat
Jasper, Yellow	forehead, mid-chest
Jet	throat, wrist
Lapis Lazuli	throat
Lazulite	finger, heart
Magnetite	anywhere
Moonstone	finger
Opal, Dark	finger, throat
Opal, Jelly	anywhere
Opal, Light	throat
Pearl	navel
Peridot	throat
Petrified Wood	throat

Pyrite	throat
Quartz, Amythest	anywhere
Quartz, Blue	finger
Quartz, Citrine	anywhere
Quartz, Clear	anywhere
Rhodochrosite	wrist
Rhodonite	throat
Ruby	heart, middle of the chest, finger, ankle
Sapphire	finger
Silver	finger
Star Sapphire	finger
Topaz	finger
Turquoise	anywhere

MENTAL AND EMOTIONAL INFLUENCES OF CRYSTALS

Agate	All agates strengthen the effect of other stones.
Agate, Botswana	Eases depression, promotes joy, dispels lethargy, increases practicality
Agate, Fire	Restores emotional balance and harmony, increases practicality, subdues sexual conflict
Agate, Moss	Eases depression, restores emotional and mental balance
Agate, Picture	Decreases apathy, sharpens mental clarity

Alexanderite	Brings happiness, increases self-esteem
Amber	Eases stress, improves decision-making, encourages eccentric behavior, strengthens memory
Apatite	Eases stress, facilitates expression, dispels nervous tension
Aquamarine	Diminishes disorientation, facilitates expression, curbs unnatural fear, sharpens mental clarity
Aventurine	Eases stress, restores emotional balance, promotes independence, sharpens mental clarity
Azurite	Improves decision-making, eases depression, heightens dreams, promotes mental balance, sharpens mental clarity, increases mental discipline and sensitivity
Azurite/ Malachite	Dispels stress, overcomes lack of discipline, heightens dreams, restores emotional balance, extends patience
Beryl	Relieves stress, overcomes laziness, strengthens mental

	balance, increases mental clarity and mental discipline, protects the wearer
Bloodstone	Encourages caution, courage, promotes mental balance and clarity, strengthens mental discipline, aids in self-actualization
Chalcedony	Soothes depression, heightens dreams, promotes goodwill, dispels irritability, brings joy and happiness, supports mental balance, increases mental clarity, reduces negativity and nightmares
Chrysocolla	Relieves stress, restores emotional balance, assuages guilt, promotes maturity, dissipates nervous tension
Chrysolite	Exposes delusion, fights depression, supports emotional and mental balance, aids in discovering past-life experience
Chrysophase	Encourages caution, improves flexibility, inhibits greed and hysteria, promotes imagination, sharpens perception and mental

	clarity, aids in recall of past-life experience
Coral	Eases depression, restores emotional balance, improves expressiveness, strengthens mental clarity, rights mental imbalances, banishes nightmares
Diamond	Dispels stress, guards against envy, relieves insecurity, improves clarity, increases self-esteem
Diopside	Relieves insecurity, strengthens self-esteem
Emerald	Restores emotional balance, aids working closely with others, facilitates expression
Fluorite	Diminishes stress
Garnet	Promotes imagination, guards against nightmares, improves self-esteem
Hematite	Improves self-esteem
Ivory	Eases frustration
Jade	Brings peace and calm, intensifies expressive ability
Jasper	Reduces stress, promotes endurance
Jet	Reduces stress, relieves depression, adds excitability, fights

	manic-depressive behavior
Lapis Lazuli	Improves expression, eases stress, dispels depression
Lazulite	Strengthens courage
Loadstone	Promotes expression, relieves insomnia
Malachite	Dispels stress, heightens expression
Moonstone	Resists mental imbalance, improves intuition and receptivity
Onyx	Relieves stress, fights depression, soothes fear
Obsidian	Wards off negativity and over-sensitivity
Opal	Promotes creativity, love, and joy, resists emotional imbalance
Pearl	Brings peace, reduces over-sensitivity
Peridot	Extends patience, sharpens clarity, calms nerves
Pyrite	Eases stress and frustration, dispels depression and anxiety
Rhodochrosite	Promotes self-love and acceptance, strengthens self-identity
Quartz, Amythest	Refreshes intuition and creativity, strengthens courage, guards against excess

Quartz, Blue	Improves creativity, has a calming influence
Quartz, Citrine	Reinforces self-confidence, the will, and creativity
Quartz, Rose	Increases confidence, heightens personal expression, creativity, and comfort
Quartz, Smoky	Improves creativity, enhances joy, balances emotions
Quartz, White	Promotes healing, works as an energizer
Ruby	Reinforces confidence, increases flexibility, vitality, and leadership skills
Sapphire	Works as a mood elevator, improves communication, dispels stress
Sodalite	Fosters harmony, courage, and communication
Star Sapphire	Enriches communication
Tiger's Eye	Gets rid of unwanted emotion, balances material and physical needs
Topaz	Enchances creativity, relaxes, balances emotions
Tourmaline, Black	Energizes
Blue	Improves communication

Green	Develops feelings of love and compassion, renews creativity
Pink	Sharpens insight and perception, strengthens creativity
Watermelon	Stimulates other tourmalines
Turquoise	Builds strength, provides protection, helps communication

CRYSTALS TO HELP YOU IN YOUR PROFESSION

A crystal can enhance the skills you need everyday on your job. Whether you have to be good at communicating precise details or grand concepts, a well chosen stone will aid you. You may have an occupation that requires good coordination, or you may operate in an environment that is often stressful. In any case, whatever you do, there's a crystal for you. The following chart lists some major occupations and the crystals that complement them. If your specific job is not here, you shouldn't have too much trouble figuring out from the entries for related jobs which crystals can help you.

Careers or Role	Crystal
Advertising	Amber, Lace Agate, Apatite, Garnet, Jasper, Lapis Lazuli

Agent	Moonstone, Ruby, Turquoise
Artist	Chrysocolla, Coral, Moonstone, Dark Opal, Blue Quartz, Rose Quartz, Pink Tourmaline
Athlete	Bloodstone, Coral, Diamond, Hematite, Magnetite, Onyx, Petrified Wood
Child Care	Chalcedony, Coral, Hematite, Malachite, Rose Quartz, Topaz
Chiropractor	Albite, Amber, Azurite, Carnelian, Chrysocolla Coral, Jade, Jasper, Jet, Lapis Lazuli, Magnetite, Petrified Wood, Pyrite
Communications: T.V. and Radio	Lace Agate, Aventurine, Garnet, Jade, Jasper, Lapis Lazuli, Malachite, Tiger's Eye
Counselor	Emerald, Magnetite, Moonstone, Ruby, Sapphire, Green Tourmaline
Dancer	Picture Agate, Amethyst, Emerald, Malachite, Pearl
Dentist	Agate, Coral, Chrysolite, Diamond, Fluorite, Jet, Lapis Lazuli, Magnetite, Malachite
Executive	Agate, Bloodstone, Carnelian, Jasper, Lapis

	Lazuli, Malachite, Moonstone, Onyx, Sard, Sardonyx
Exterminator	Jet, Smoky Quartz, Turquoise
Farmer, Gardener	Moss Agate, Amber, Amethyst, Coral, Diamond, Emerald, Jadeite, Moonstone, Pearl
Guards, Police	Bloodstone, Carnelian, Jasper, Jet, Moonstone, Onyx, Sard, Sardonyx
Homemaker	Chalcedony, Coral, Chrysoprase, Garnet, Emerald, Moonstone, Rose Quartz, Topaz
Management	Agate, Chrysocolla, Jade, Jasper, Lazulite, Petrified Wood, Rose Quartz, Sard, Turquoise
Midwife	Moss Agate, Amazonite, Beryl, Chalcedony, Jade, Moonstone, Pink Tourmaline
Musician	Chrysocolla, Jade, Lazulite
Optometrist	Agate, Aquamarine, Adventurine, Beryl, Diopside, Emerald, Hematite, Jade, Kunzite, Opal
Politician	Jade, Jasper, Moonstone, Sard, Sardonyx, Turquoise
Professor	Amethyst, Amber, Malachite, Pearl, Rose

	Quartz, Sapphire, Turquoise
Sales	Lace Agate, Coral, Moonstone, Petrified Wood
Scientist	Azurite, Calcite, Diamond, Fluorite, Jasper, Lapis Lazuli, Pyrite
Singer	Aquamarine, Chrysocolla, Emerald
Student	Beryl, Diamond, Enstatite, Lapis Lazuli, Rose Quartz
Surgeon	Diamond, Fluorite, Magnetite, Malachite
Teacher	Lace Agate, Pyrite, Rose Quartz, Turquoise
Veterinarian	Coral, Jasper, Petrified Wood, Rose Quartz, Turquoise
Word Processor	Lace Agate, Emerald, Lapis Lazuli, Malachite, Turquoise

---

GLOSSARY

Atlantis Mythical, technologically advanced society that was supposedly destroyed many centuries ago.

Auric Field A low-level energy field that surrounds the body. It gives off a dim glow that is often a single color from the light spectrum. This field is not visible to the average person but some of its effects can be recorded with Kirlian photography.

Birthstone Stones assigned to individuals born during a specific month of the year. Historically, these stones were chosen for superstitious or religious reasons for the purpose of protection. Also called natal stones.

Centering The process of feeling solid and focused in your emotional nature.

Cleansing System Organs that filter or detoxify the body. Includes liver, kidneys, pancreas, spleen, appendix, lymph glands.

Elestial Crystals Crystals that are young in terms of geological time. These crystals are generally quite small in size with blunt ends.

Elixirs Elixirs are made by placing a crystal or gemstone in a glass of water for a period of up to seven hours. The stone is removed and the elixir imbibed. This liquid is said to carry the stone's essence or low-level vibrational energy. It is seen as an immediate solution to internal physical problems and to be used in addition to healing layouts.

Grounding Developing a sense of security; the ability to feel comfortable about people and situations that surround you.

Mental Plane   Mental perception, the thought process. Conscious or unconscious acknowledgment of your existence.

Physical Plane   Through coordination with the mental plane, the acknowledgment of all physical sensation and the workings of all organs and systems of the body.

Pyramid   Geometric shape that creates an energy field within itself possessing regenerative powers for objects placed inside it. Often pyramids are made out of copper.

Spiritual Plane   One's personal perceptions regarding the existence of life after death, the theories regarding the creation of all existing life, the belief in a single entity as God, and the existence of a collective consciousness.

Talisman   Anything used for intuitive reasons to ward off negative energy or influences. Often religion or superstition is involved, though a talisman can be as simple as a favorite hat or good luck charm.